THE
REMOVAL MEN

MICK LYNCH

NEWMAN SPRINGS PUBLISHING
320 Broad Street
Red Bank, NJ 07701

First originally published by Newman Springs Publishing 2018

ISBN 978-1-64096-408-2 (Paperback)
ISBN 978-1-64096-409-9 (Digital)

This is a creative work of nonfiction that best captures the details as I recall them. Identifying details have been changed to protect people's privacy. The names I have used are those of my friends and family who have been asked to be included for better or worse.

Some names have been added to please those individuals so I will be included in their wills!

Illustrations by Paige E. Mulhern
Paige.Mulhern@MassArt.edu

Printed in the United States of America

This book is dedicated to
Nan, Mum, Dad, Jan, Hillary and Phil

Contents

Introduction

As a teenage boy, I would write poems. Some were mine and some I stole from song lyrics and mixed the two together. I wasn't trying to plagiarize anybody; it was just an exercise for me to enhance my style. I would write comical letters to debt collector agencies when they screwed up my accounts. As I got older, I wrote them for my friends to newspapers just to see if they would publish them. The funny thing about newspapers is that they have a style of letter-writing they expect from the public and that's what gets printed. When I learned that style, I would write all kinds of letters, sometimes for my amusement and occasionally for a profitable advantage; for example, when I wrote a fake angry letter to my local newspaper and received two complementary tickets to a game of my beloved Coventry City Football Club in the Director's Box for the next time I was in England. I have heard there is a book in everyone, but I had resigned myself to the fact that, as good as I thought my imagination was, I could not think of a scenario that would fill more than a dozen pages. I could make people laugh by making fun of myself or talking about things that went through my head that many people tend to keep bottled up inside for the sake of embarrassment or sanity. In fact, when I look back at all the things I had written, I realized they were all based on reality. I have had many jobs over the past forty years, just like the lyrics from an old blues song. I left school on a Friday and started working on a Monday at fifteen years of age. I have been a printer, a drummer in a psychedelic band, a resident DJ in a hippie pub, a painter, a construction worker, and a designer, all of which had their moments but nothing to write about until I literally stumbled onto this job. I hope you enjoy reading it as much as I enjoyed living it.

Vampires, Ghosts, and the Church

"Michael, Michael, get up. We'll be late! What is the matter with that child?" my grandmother says.

"There's nothing wrong with me, Nana. I don't want to go!" I say to myself as I slap my slippers on the floor to make her think I am out of bed.

Where is it that I don't want to go? Mass. This one in particular is a requiem Mass. I'm a good Catholic boy, but after all I'm only ten. What do I know? Well, I know this. My religion tells me that when you are dead, you leave this world: if you were good, you go to heaven; and if you were bad, you go to hell. You can't come back to life and there are no such things as ghosts, but when we go to Mass, I am told that the son of God died and rose from the dead three days later and we pray to God, the Holy Ghost. I just don't get it!

Anyway, back to more pressing matters. When we go to Communion, I have to walk past a real live coffin. Oh God, what if I brush it with my clothes or worse with my bare arm? My nana knows this.

"Get up!" she yells again.

Remember the dead can't hurt you; it's only the living. Oh really? And what about Dracula? He's dead but he still goes around biting people, and then they die and come back to life at night. What if the person in the coffin is one of those? This fear of the dead, the undead and all of America's Hollywood and England's Hammer Horror Productions weird and wonderful creatures stayed with me up to middle age. I've never seen *The Exorcist,* Freddy, or any of the fright movies. I can watch suspense movies because I know, more often than not, there is nothing around the corner of the dark room, but in the horror films there always is. So how is it that forty years later I am cradling the head of a dead Dorchester boy who has been shot through the head in a drive-by shooting in Lynn?

2

New Neighbors

Well, it happened like this. Our quiet little street in Marblehead has one rental house, so people move in and out about every other year or so. As I look out my window one Saturday morning, the new people arrive in two minivans; what looks to me like a husband and wife in their mid-forties, two kids, and an older guy. The husband seems be the one giving out all the orders military-style. Maybe he is a former sergeant or something. A couple of days later, I notice two of the minivans have numbered license plates with the word *Hearse* underneath.

"Oh god, are you kidding me?" I think as I shudder by.

The vans are owned by Phil Handley and his wife Julie. The older guy turns out to be Harry, Phil's number 2. Phil has an embalming and body-removal business called TRE (Trade Removals and Embalmings). He contracts with funeral homes where he will pick up the deceased, takes them to a specific funeral home, and then, in most cases, embalm the body. The Boston Medical Examiner's Office employs him in a similar process, but in those cases he is picking them up from accident and crime scenes, homicides, suicides, and "we're just not sure-icides." Any suspicious or unexpected deaths end up at the ME's office.

After working for a print finishing company for ten years, I became self-employed. I have an interior painting company and I design and build English/Irish pubs, sports bars, man caves (and, for that matter, woman caves), wines bars, etc., in people's homes. So, when I'm not working for myself during the day, I hang out at Phil's, which is not usually for very long as the phone calls come in at regular intervals.

July 4th Celebration

Phil and I become fast friends. He is a very likeable and organized character, generous to a fault. He can take the most reserved people and turn them into party animals, for a short while anyway. July 4th is here and Phil is having a party at his home. The mix of people at the gathering is astounding and from every walk of life. It's like his own private collection of characters, Phil's human menagerie, if you will: politicians, mega-rich gay men, police, firemen, couples, singles, and some characters you wouldn't want to turn your back on (oh sorry, I already mentioned politicians, didn't I?). We are well into July 5th now and with only Phil and I standing (me, barely), he asks me if I would like to go out on a case with him. It's 3:00 a.m. and I have been drinking that black-bodied, cream-headed liquid imported from Ireland by the pint all night long, so I am up for pretty much anything.

"Sure," I said.

"When do we start?"

"We have to get a phone call first, Mick."

"Oh. Okay." I leave Phil's at 3:30 a.m. and go to my house next door.

Fancy a Trip to the Seaside?

It's 3:33 a.m. There is a knock on the door below.

"Come on, Mick. Drive-by shooting on Lynn Beach. Put on good pants and a shirt. Let's go!"

An instant adrenalin rush goes through me. I am not drunk anymore. As I get in the hearse, he says we are going to Dunkin Donuts.

"Grab a coffee, eat some mints, and don't breathe on the policemen."

I remember it as being a mixture of trepidation and overwhelming excitement. My wife, however, remembers it differently. She recalls that in the middle of the night, all of the bedroom lights went on and shoes and clothing came flying out of the closet. She described me as being barely able to stand and dress myself.

"What do I have to do?"

"You're the ankle man," he said smiling. Just follow my lead.

We arrive at the scene. The road is cordoned off. I see the look on the officer's face. We are in an unmarked minivan. It doesn't say Phil's body pickup service or *Have body, will travel*. It just has that little license plate with *Hearse* on it. The officer looks like he has been turning people away for a while now. As we pull up, I can see he is about to tell us to make a U-turn or words to that effect. When Phil tells me to yell to him "ME's office," his growl turns into a smile.

"Right through, guys," he says.

They're always happy to see us. It means they can leave soon. There are state troopers, local police, the fire department, and detectives there. The scene is ablaze with blue and red flashing lights, news media, cameras everywhere, onlookers, and a helicopter overhead. My god, this is CS-freaking-I Miami, Lynn style.

That would be the only part of the operation that would resemble the glitzy TV show as I would find out upon on our arrival at the ME's office.

"We are going to be in and out of here in five minutes," says Phil as we pull up and open the back of the van.

He shows me where the release handles of the stretcher are, and he grabs a body bag and two sets of gloves.

"Just follow my lead. We will put the stretcher next to the door. I will pull him out, lay him down, zip the bag up, and we will be gone."

Okay, Phil, as long as I don't have to touch him, I think. The boy is sitting in the driver's seat of the car. We lower the stretcher (at least I didn't screw that up), and the body bag is unzipped and opened. I wonder how we will get him out of the car. Won't he be stiff?

Phil grabs him by his T-shirt and pulls him out.

"Hold his head," he says.

"Who, me?"

He must be mistaking me for someone who doesn't mind touching dead bodies, but there is no time to do anything but react to his command. Both hands went under his head and we laid him down gently on the open body bag.

"We don't want there to be any postmortem bruising before the autopsy."

Of course we don't, Phil, I quipped to myself, like I should know this. We zipped up the bag. I took the ankle end and lifted the stretcher. The kid only weighed about 110 pounds. I would soon realize why weight was important. We wheeled him to the van, slid him in the door, shut it, and we were gone. It couldn't have taken more than four minutes. Phil is so proficient that he made me look good.

"Mick," he quipped, "your coffee didn't even get cold."

He's talking to me like we have just picked up takeout or something. Doesn't he realize there's a dead body behind us and it's nudging the back of my seat every time we brake for traffic?

The Boston ME's Office

We arrive at the medical examiner's office. It is around the back of a busy downtown location. It's not busy now as it is 4:30 a.m. We bring the body in through the metal roll up door. There is a reception room desk and a pair of rubber doors.

"Hey, Phil. Is this the Lynn shooting?" says a fifty-something man.

"Yes, Dale. This is Mick."

"Ah, your latest recruit."

By this time, I had already discovered the Hollywood part was over. This was not *Crossing Jordan* or CSI anything. No soft orange, blue, and pink lights bathing the building for that relaxed ambiance. No devilishly handsome men or beautiful woman with low-cut tops and ample bosoms looking for that one hair that could prove it was indeed a homicide, not an accident. This was a stark, colorless room warmed only by the wit and humor of the people who worked there. After checking him in, he is fingerprinted and a photo is taken of his head. All of the body photos were done back at the scene. He is then taken through the rubber doors, stripped of his clothes, and rolled onto the scales. All present take a guess at the weight.

"I win," says Patty.

The little things, I suppose, make one's day in this business. He is then zipped back up to await the autopsy.

There are numerous rooms off this corridor, cold rooms where the bodies are kept, rooms with body parts, some marked in cardboard boxes, and some marked with the words *baby parts* on them. This is quite a lot to take in on my first night, or so I thought at the time, my "one-off experience." I roll into bed about 6:00 a.m. I have difficulty sleeping. The adrenaline is still pumping, but Phil has a cure for that.

6

Hanging Around in the Park

"Mick Lynch," I hear from the street below. It's 8 a.m. on the very same day!

"Let's go. Suicide hanging in Groton and it's in public view."

This means we need to get there as quick as possible as he can be seen openly by the public. I struggle into my clothes, pants, and a collared shirt. No one wants to see their loved ones picked up by a pair of guys in T-shirts, shorts, and baseball caps, although, in this humidity, you wish you could sometimes. He is very much in the open as it turned out; he had hung himself from a footbridge. By the time we got there, the fire department had cut him down and put him in one of their basket stretchers with a sheet over him. They had left the scene leaving only a lone police officer. We can't take the basket, so the officer calls them to come back and pick it up. I am standing by the head. Good, his head is covered. I don't have to see him. As that thought goes through my head, Phil bends down and pulls the sheet back quickly. The man stares back at me, the rope still attached to his neck.

"You asshole," I say.

"What?" says Phil. "I just wanted to see his neck jewelry."

And he is my friend, why? Back to Boston and the drop-off is done.

I am sorry to say that I can't remember the next four cases that made up that week. Phil told me this would happen, but I had so righteously told him how I would never forget any of them.

There were so many that they began to run together in the beginning. To avoid forgetting any more, I began to write down the towns and cities on paper as well as little notes if they were unusual cases, otherwise the details were fading away.

The Numbers Game

As I start to write this account, I am three months into it and have removed forty bodies. This is on a night-time and weekend basis as I have a full-time job. I have no idea how many Phil has picked up. By the time I picked up my sixth body, I had lost my fear of the dead completely. Nana was right. Only the living can hurt you, and I had seen this to be oh so true on a number of occasions. This is a business like any other, so I hope that you understand when I say that we are paid by the body, so the more bodies we get, the more money we make. (Not that you can drum up business if it's not there!)

We have our own area that we cover. Phil has from the border of Boston on the North Shore up to Rockport and the New Hampshire border. His wife asked me one day if I was still excited about going to the high-profiles scenes.

"Yes," I said. "How about you?"

"I'm over it," she retorted.

My wife doesn't want to hear any of the gory details, but my young daughter does.

"Daddy, I saw you on TV again tonight." She beams with pride.

8

Nightmares and Other Fun Stuff

"How do you sleep at night?" I get asked.

"Very well, actually," I reply (mostly due to exhaustion).

They are, of course, referring to nightmares of which I have had only one. I was sitting at a table with the first six "bodies" I had picked up, talking to them about their lives and the afterlife. Everything was going fine with me thinking how great it was that I could talk to them about all this stuff and how happy they are. Now I can go back and tell their families everything and help them achieve closure. Wow! How marvelous am I?

"Well, it was great talking with you guys. I can't believe I was able to do this."

"Well, we're all dead," one replied.

"Yes, I know," I said. "Okay. Maybe we can do this again."

"Of course, we can. We're all dead."

"Yes, good. Maybe next year."

"Sure, next year . . . the year after . . . the century after . . . whenever you want Mick! *We're all dead!*"

That woke me up in a hot sweat. I never had that dream again!

Four Months In

By the fourth month, I have the basics down and Phil gives me a raise. He tells me that I have actually become a help to him now. So far there is nothing noteworthy to report, just regular pickups, but that was about to change.

I have been to a couple of embalmings and thought long and hard about whether or not I should explain how they work. I decided against it at this time.

There are two sayings in this industry that are very commonly used. One is "no love, no loss." When you think about receiving news concerning the death of someone you don't know well or someone who is a distant relative you barely knew, or even a movie or rock star, you might be surprised or even slightly shocked, but it's not devastating. The other saying is "there's no dignity in death." By that I am not talking about when a loved one has drawn their last breath. I mean the process that follows once the body has been removed and in the funeral home to give you what you see when they are finally in the casket and ready to be waked. The other thing I could never say is "Sorry for your loss." The reason for that may be because I heard it so often it seemed almost meaningless and insincere. I know you have to say something, but it just sounded so mechanical to me.

10

The Grand Old Game

It's my daughter's friend's birthday. The whole street has been invited and parents and kids are running everywhere trying to coordinate rides for us all to go to a North Shore Spirits minor league baseball game in Lynn. Phil and I take the hearse even though it is only one town over from ours. You couldn't have asked for a more beautiful summer evening.

We settle down to watch, beer in one hand, hot dog in the other, and of course, right on cue, one bite, one sip, and Phil's cell phone rings. A gentleman, Ray, had been using his estranged wife as target practice. She had returned to the house to pick up the remainder of her clothes and he had taken several potshots at her in the street. Fortunately, he had missed and, after a three-hour siege with the SWAT team, had turned the shotgun on himself. One of the things you have to be proficient at in this job is map-reading. Some locations are very difficult to find, and many houses don't have street numbers displayed clearly. Also, many streets are not signposted. Once you are on the street, you are usually okay because there is bound to be at least one cruiser there and, more often than not, a whole stage show of blue and red lights. But here's the thing. How often has someone asked you where so-and-so road is and you know it but can't remember exactly where it is and it turns out to be two streets from where you have lived for the past ten years? That was our situation with this address as we spent twenty minutes going up and down the same streets asking neighbors. No one knew. Finally I ask about the shooting and right away I was directed "over there" as they point to the street opposite where they are all standing.

We arrive at the scene, which appears to be a major deal: a SWAT team, police, detectives, fire department, news stations, helicopters, and neighbors. Everyone is here. Phil tells me that this could be messy, but messy couldn't prepare me for what I was about to see.

We are directed to the unfinished basement. As we enter, there is a small office on the far side of the room. The door is open and in between all the people milling around, I get a glimpse of him. He is sitting in a swivel chair. I can't see his face at first as it appears his head is all the way back. There is a good reason for that. Most of it has been blown away.

"A shotgun barrel in the mouth will do that," Phil quips.

This is the first case I have been to where I feel no remorse for the deceased. As I enter the room behind Phil, he tells me to stop.

"We need hazmat suits," he says, "And biohazard bags, maybe half a dozen."

We all have these bags at home. They are called freezer bags, but if you print the biohazard symbol and the accompanying word *biohazard* on them, they are BIOHAZARD bags. We suit up and he asks me if I want brains or skull.

"Yeah right, Phil." I laugh, but my friend Phil isn't laughing.

"Oh well, er, I don't know." It's not like the choice is onion rings or French fries.

"Brains" apparently comes out of my mouth.

There is water dripping from the ceiling, or so my ears are telling me. My eyes are telling me a different scenario. As we enter the room, the force of the shotgun has created a macabre scene. There is blood, skull, and brains all over the walls and dripping from the ceiling. He is a big boy weighing about 300 pounds. We slide him easily off of the chair, into the body bag, and remove him from the small office. We don't take him upstairs yet as we still have to fill our biohazard bags. Phil tells me we must find all of the body remains as we don't want family members to come across fragments after we have left. Now I know that brains are a delicacy in some countries, and I had wondered how people could touch them, never mind eat them. Well, I was about to find out what it was like to touch them.

I thought brains were gray probably because of the frequent reference to them as gray matter. I thought that they would have a texture like polystyrene or that fake dirt that they put in little plant pots. They are neither. They are pink and white in color and have a texture like soft velvet.

"What about the blood?" I ask.

"That's not our problem," he says. "There are companies who do that."

"Good." I think.

We put the freezer bags in with the body and get him up the rickety basement stairs with a little difficulty, mainly on my part, as I have not lifted a body this heavy before. If only I knew what I would encounter in the future. Meanwhile, the SWAT team has found boxes and boxes of ammunition and five or six shotguns, handguns, and the most startlingly depraved and graphic porn sites on his computer. Oh yes, and a drawer full of ladies panties. In fairness to him, with his wife gone, he probably didn't have any clean underwear of his own! By the time we drop him back in Boston, the baseball game is over.

Proper Attire

Let's talk about dress attire for a minute. I have already explained about the shirt and pants, and in a lot of cases, rubber gloves are the only other accessories required. We are usually told in advance if hazmat suits are required or if the victim/s has, or may have, HIV, hep C, or any other transmittable diseases. There is an exception to the rule requirement of rubber gloves. On occasion, we pick up a body where there are clearly no suspicious circumstances and, for the sake of the on-looking family, wearing gloves may appear to look like their loved one is somehow unclean or contagious. Respect is very important in these sensitive times. We have to check the clothes of the deceased for personal belongings. Jewelry and money need to be counted, witnessed, and photographed, and of course we need to be very careful of needles as the last thing we need is to accidently get pricked by an infected one. Why so much formality over belongings? If we didn't do this, there would be nothing stopping family members from asking (and they have in the past) where Uncle Scott's wad of hundred-dollar bills has disappeared to or Aunt Kathy's $510,000 ring, a family heirloom "don't 'cha know."

Party Drugs

OxyContin has become the drug of the day. I know it was originally intended to help relieve the pain of the terminally ill in their final stages, but it has become so easily available that its misuse has become an epidemic. Keep in mind that I am writing this account many years after these chronicled events; I know that drugs such as OxyContin have become more difficult to obtain.

For my first OxyContin party, we are back in Revere. Two males and one female are partying. The female's young teenage son is also present. The son (who is not high) tells his mother that one of the males is on the floor and is turning blue while the other male is frothing from the mouth. He wants to call for help.

"Yes, go for help. Call the police. They are in serious trouble," says the mother.

Oh, hang on! No she didn't! She is also as high as a kite and tells him he is going nowhere and that they will be all right.

"We don't want the police coming here."

The boy ignores her, gets out of the apartment, finds a working pay phone, and calls for help. His common sense probably saved his mother, definitely saved one of the males, but it is too late for the red-haired Irish boy on the kitchen floor.

13

Keeping Things in Order

I considered grouping these events into neat little categories: drugs, traffic accidents, homicides, etc., but having read through my notes, it wouldn't have made sense to do this as my comments and opinions changed the more cases I handled.

I had considered Phil to be very hardnosed and embittered in some cases, not that he ever showed any evidence of this at any of the scenes. He is a true professional, always in control, but by the end of my first year, I was becoming somewhat hardened, but not all the time as there were many sad and tragic cases.

I was back at home for an hour and the next call comes in. It is a straightforward case this time. A lady has died at her home and the funeral home wants us to take the body to the local hospital. We arrive and are met by the brother who asks us if we can give him a couple of minutes alone with her. The apartment door opens and in walks, or staggers, her very drunk boyfriend. He goes into the bedroom and after a couple of minutes, we ask them if they could go into the living room while we prepare her. The brother leaves but not the boyfriend. He is rambling and muttering and is sitting on the floor next to her. It's not because he is traumatized but rather because he is so inebriated he just can't stand up.

As we are leaving, a new call comes in from the ME's office concerning an apartment fire in Lowell with two possible fatalities. We can't get three stretchers in the van, so we need to drop the woman off quickly to make room for the new bodies.

Fires and Heroes

Now there are apparently rules about driving on the roads in Massachusetts, although if you have driven in Massachusetts at all, you may be forgiven for thinking there aren't any! Speed limits, one-way streets, staying on the road and not the sidewalks, are just some simple rules that we don't abide by when we are in a hurry.

We drop off the female and head up quickly to Lowell. When we arrive, we are told that they have saved one person and the dead male is on the second floor. The building has been gutted by the fire. There is water cascading down through the floors. It is nighttime and there is no working electricity in the building. The floor is covered in burnt wood. The mix of water and charcoaled wood has made the floor like black papier-mache and with all the fire hoses on the floor, it is very difficult to keep your balance. We need not have hurried, as it turned out, because firemen are checking every apartment for the possibility of occupants. A large group has gathered and a few individuals are staring at us. They don't know if there are any fatalities, but they are sensing that we are hanging around for a reason other than morbid curiosity.

"How the hell are we going to get him down from there, Phil? It will be a nightmare."

"Let's see what the firemen say," he says confidently.

Having been in similar situations before, he is well aware of how amazing firemen are. The chief comes over and tells us that we are clear to go in.

"It's very dangerous in there, guys. Would you like me to get my guys to bring him down to floor level?"

"That would be great, chief," says Phil as he gives me a wink (freakin' know it all).

Now we were not under any circumstances looking to get out of this (okay, I was). If we had to go in, we would have, but firemen are a breed apart and Phil knows this. Allowing them to bring the body down will be far quicker than us doing it, and it will help disburse the large crowd that has gathered. Why it took 9/11 for firemen to be called heroes is beyond me! The guy was on the stairwell in the fetal position and had died of smoke inhalation. He was completely blackened not from the flames but from the searing heat which had literally fused him in that position. Back to Boston and bed in the wee hours of the morning.

15

Surfing USA

It's Sunday morning and we are on our way to Malden. It is an extremely humid New England day. There are three of us today as the guy we are removing is close to 400 pounds. We arrive at the YMCA. He is up on the fourth floor of what must have been a beautiful hotel in its day. The stairs are very wide, which is a good thing, but steep, which is a bad thing. We have a backboard, I'm sure you have seen them on TV—bright orange. They look like a surfboard and for good reason because that is how we are going to get him down. We will slide him all the way to the bottom. We have to use two body bags to cover him, and he is secured tightly to the backboard as is often the case with large, overweight people. He has a huge belly, which tends to move from side to side like Jell-o, causing a balancing problem for us. Phil and Big Harry are the brake men at the back of the board, and I am at the front. They are strapped to the backboard so as to hold the heavy body from careening down the stairs, and I am steering. We are at the top of the stairs. The policemen are watching.

"This I've got to see," says one of them.

If they slip or the straps break, I am toast and the body surfs down on its own or crashes through the wall. Ten grueling minutes later, we are down, safe and sound, much to the admiration of the attending officers.

Myths and Truths

There are a number of misconceptions about what happens to the human body right after death. Rigor mortis does not set in immediately; it takes about twelve hours. After about the same period of time, it disappears again. If you have heard stories about funeral assistants having to break the bones of people in order to get them in the body bag or coffin when found dead in unusual positions (and by that I mean not lying flat and not what might be going through your minds), there were none on my watch, although I am sure there have been plenty of people who have been found in compromising positions, but I am getting off point. When a body is found in rigor, we have to pump the arms or legs like you would to jack up a car. This allows the blood to artificially flow and the appendages to lay flat so no bone breaks.

Do bodies exhale breath after death? *Yes!* A buildup of gases can cause exhalation, especially if the body is being moved around. Even hours later, the buildup can cause it to look like it is exhaling. That's always a little bit of fun for us, especially if there is a rookie cop on the scene at his or her first death.

Do people lose bowel control when they die? *No!* Generally speaking, this could happen if, in fact, they were engaged in that activity at the time of death, but not as a rule. It is also a possibility if the deceased sees their demise coming, they could, quite literally, be scared shitless.

They Won't Find Me Here

People have weird ideas of what they consider to be safe places to do drugs. That statement alone makes me smile. If you want to be safe, don't do them; but let's just say people ignore that advice. In a car, a dark parking lot, or on your own with no one around to see you—all seem to be very popular and safe venues from busybodies like neighbors and police. That is, until it all goes wrong and there is no one there to help you because no one knows you are there. Then, of course, it's those damn pain-in-the-ass cops who eventually find you and Phil and me who take you on your final car ride.

She Looks So Peaceful

Hospitals and nursing homes are the cases that are the least physically taxing for us. In the hospitals, the bodies are most always already prepared for pickup in the hospital morgue. In the nursing homes, most of the time, the old people are in bed when they pass and we take them from there. Although there is less exertion required, they can present other challenges. Security guards at hospitals are the bane of our profession, not all of them, but as you will read from these accounts, more than enough.

We are off to a nursing home in Peabody. It's just past midnight and the nurse tells us that Ms. Saucier is in 213 by the window. As we enter the room, there are four old ladies *all* by the window, all lying on their backs with their mouths wide open and barely a noticeable breath among them, three of which are resting peacefully and one resting in peace.

"Christ, Phil, which one is it?"

"Poke that one in the eye, Mick, and see if she moves."

I didn't, but I think the jerk knew all along which one it was.

19

Decos

Decomposing bodies, oh joy! My first deco! Phil had told me sooner or later we would be picking one up, so sooner it is! We arrive in Malden. The house has no electricity. It is about 9: 30 p.m.

"Why are the cops standing outside?" I ask. "It's not that warm."

"It's the smell." He grins.

How bad can it be? I've smelled skunk, rotting garbage, stink bombs. Well, to paraphrase Bachman Turner Overdrive, "You ain't smelled nothin' yet." As we enter the house, this odious, nauseating smell washes over us.

"What do you think, Mick?"

"Wanker" is my endearing reply.

There are a couple of things you can do to alleviate the smell: put a vapor rub under your nose; wear an expensive breathing apparatus (wearing a regular contractor's mask will do nothing); breathe it in which will eventually, for most people, make you throw up; or what we do as I learned this day was to talk and breathe through your mouth. I was partially successful with this on the first couple of times and eventually got the hang of it. An officer has called the local fire department and they are on their way with lighting. We have flashlights to survey the scene. The house is a pit: takeout food all over the floor, empty booze and soda cans, newspapers, junk mail going back years, and garbage bags spilt open everywhere. Well, the owner may be dead, but there are things inside the garbage bags that are not. We are told by the detective that there is a suspicion of "foul" play, quite an ironic choice of words.

"If he is in the room, he is well hidden," I say to Phil.

There is always (for me anyway) a moment of nervous anticipation before you see the body. After all, I am in a dark room and there is going to be something around the comer, and who knows what state they are going to be in? After a few more seconds, our eyes have adjusted to the dark and the flashlights and I see him.

"There's Liberace," I say.

Yes, that came out of my mouth and not Phil's. The man is stuck down the side of a grand piano. It surprised me that one of the worst pits I have ever been in had a grand piano in the living room. The firemen arrive with the lighting, and when it is all is set up, I get my first look at a deco. With our white hazmat suits on, we look more like we are going for a walk on the moon. We clear the various objects that came crashing down on him at that fatal moment, and with the piano out of the way we get our first good look at him. He has been there for at least three days, and as we pump the various limbs to get him flat, Phil tells me to be careful that he doesn't explode. Explode? Really, Phil? What he meant was that after a certain amount of time, the skin becomes very thin and translucent and can burst. The guy is every shade of purple through black. We have to turn him over onto his side so pictures can be taken of his back to make sure that there are no bullet holes or knife wounds, or actual knives, for that matter. This is called a trauma roll. As we lay him on the body bag, all of that pumping of his limbs takes its toll and he oozes blood out of his mouth.

If you are wondering why I haven't run screaming from the house by now with my track record, I'm not sure I can explain. As a kid, it is everything I imagined it would be, and here I am zipping up the body bag. One thing comes to mind after having watched all those CSI programs where they are so graphic at crime scenes and autopsies. Perhaps it has become as surreal as I have seen it all on TV and it looks just the same here. There are two vehicles missing from the victim's property, an old truck and a Jaguar. It kind of mimics the house, a pit and a grand piano. The Jaguar is found at a motel parking lot on Route 1 in Peabody, a stretch of road I would become very familiar with. We get him into the van and are trapped with that smell for another half hour. There is yet one more option to obliterating the odor and that is to smoke. Fortunately for me, Phil does.

20

Pardon the Interruption

Another YMCA, this time in Chelsea. The gent is about 300 pounds. He is, of course, on the top floor. It's midnight. The stairs are so narrow that the superintendent suggests that we take him out through the fire escape: a good alternative except for the fact that it is raining cats and dogs and the metal stairs are very slippery. We backboard him and start our descent. As we get halfway down, it appears that we have attracted an audience from the building opposite.

"Hey, they're bringing a body down," slurs one of the onlookers.

We ignore him. This building and the one opposite of it remind me of a Dickensian scene in eighteenth-century England, dark and foreboding. The shouting continues.

"Can't you take him out another way? Why should we have to witness this?"

There are five of them who have left the living room of their apartment to crane their necks out of a small window to see us.

"Get back from the window and go snort another line," retorts the detective.

It may not be PC to make comments like this, but after a while the filth, squalor, and the personal and emotional devastation that we witness every day that is caused by drugs wears thin on your patience and can make you immune to the compassion you may have once possessed.

Accident or Suicide?

This is my first accident scene. The car is not visible from the road. There is a gap in a row of hedges. A young man has sped across a main road, miraculously missing everyone on the way, but then hits a tree head-on. A witness said that he had smashed the back end of the car around a lamppost only a minute earlier and continued on driving. Did he blow his second chance at life or did it take him two attempts to kill himself?

While I understand the right to film and report such events, I see no need to try and get close-ups of, well, basically smashed or dismembered bodies going into body bags. Perhaps if it was one of their friends or family appearing on every local news channel, they would have a different point of view. Yes, I know the public has a right to know, but if they could get past their own self-importance, they would realize that there are things the majority of the public don't want to see and accident victims may be one of them. They are out of luck on this occasion as Phil has the police keep them back and two officers hold a tarp up to block the view of the cameras.

22

Tattoo Me

This morning we are off to a hospital, not the regular basement run where we go to the morgue and pick up the body from a refrigerated room, but a ward where an eighteen-year-old girl, Rose, has died of a drug overdose. Phil warns me that if the family is there, it will be very emotional and could get out of hand. When we arrive, there are two detectives outside the room.

"How are things?" asks Phil.

"Just the mother and grandmother. It should be okay," replies one of the detectives.

We enter the room to an outburst of tears. The mother doesn't want to leave her baby. Phil asks me to get gloves as this is a heroin overdose and unfortunately we don't know what we may be exposed to. I am happy to leave the room and try to calm myself down. I have been fighting back the tears. The emotion of the family and the age of the victim have, for the first time, affected me. When I return, Phil is using all of his considerable skills to get the mother to give her child one last hug before we take her away. I leave the room for the bathroom. On my way back, the detective tells me that the mother had thrown the daughter out of the house three years earlier and she had been living at a notorious crack house. When I return, the mother is telling Phil how this is the second time she has lost a loved one in the last year. Her fiancée died a week before their wedding. She then leaves Phil and I stunned as she raises the back of her T-shirt to reveal the written obituary of her fiancé tattooed from top to bottom on her back. After they leave, we have to go through the same ritual of checking personal belongings and logging them. The girl is stunning even in death. She is also naked, which makes it easier to check on jewelry. She has plenty of earrings: nose ring, tongue stud, nipple ring, piercings in her belly button and between her legs, and toe rings. In my original notes, I had blamed the mother for her child's situation, but looking back now, I don't know the details of why her mother threw her out. She could have been wild, but either way another young life has been snuffed out because of drugs.

Driving

For people who have never been in a serious car accident or seen the results first hand, I want to say this: I was recently at my daughter's drivers ed class and the instructor started to talk about the importance of wearing your seat belt when you are with a child who is learning or whom you are allegedly teaching to drive. Taking lessons with an accredited driving school in England and passing what can only be described as a challenging driving test put me in good stead for getting my license in the States, or so I thought. Never in my wildest dreams did I think it would be so easy to pass. What took an hour of intense driving back home was then followed by a ten-minute jaunt around the block when I came here. It does, of course, explain the imbecilic driving practices of the majority of the people in the state of Massachusetts. When I first started driving over here, I thought they were just vindictive, but the truth is that their driving skills are nonexistent (although some are), and yes, I use the word *skills* because real driving is a skill and should not be considered a God-given right when you reach the age of sixteen and a half. When you get behind the wheel of a car, you are responsible for everyone else on the road. That thought alone could save thousands of lives. I don't want to get on my high horse about this. I make mistakes driving—but they are mistakes; they are not the way I drive. How can you think that if you are at a four-way stop sign behind someone else with cars at the other three stops that you have the right to go next, or coming up to a rotary with signs the size of skyscrapers telling you to give way to traffic on the rotary that you drive straight onto them? Rotaries work wonderfully if the people using them are taught how to use them properly, like which lane to be in, how to use your directionals on them, and of course, how to use directionals in general. Traffic would flow better and people would get to and from their destinations quicker if people observed the rules of the road as written!

There are, of course, many more moronic practices which I won't get into as I have gone off track somewhat, and these practices contribute to the early demise of so many people. It is scandalous not to make the written test more about driving rules whereas as in my daughters' case, of the twenty questions asked, three related to driving and the other seventeen were related to such topics as how long your license will be suspended if you are caught as a deadbeat dad. This leaves me utterly speechless. Why do you need to have multiple choice questions? You either know it or you don't, and if you don't, learn it. You shouldn't pass a driving test on luck.

Getting back to my daughter's drivers ed class: As the instructor started on the seat belt conversation, three or four forty-something-year-old men in front started shaking their heads in silent disagreement. You see, these are the guys who have not been in an accident of any consequence and have been told by a friend of theirs that story about someone they knew who would be alive today had it not been for the seat belt. C'mon, you know the story! You've heard it from any one of your friends who don't wear one, the one in a million who would have been thrown clear of the accident but for the belt. The amount of lives seat belts save every year goes into the millions, and if the cost is one or two people who were unlucky enough to suffer from that fate, just do the math. I know which odds I will take.

24

Who Should Drive?

It is 3 a.m. the day after Christmas and Route 1 South just outside of Boston is closed. We arrive on the scene where there is a crushed car in the breakdown lane, a blue pickup truck in the first lane, and a green car fifty yards farther up the road with little to no apparent damage. The cameras are here and there is a helicopter overhead. This is the story of decisions made after drinking. Two guys have been at a friend's house celebrating Christmas. They decide to leave at 2:30 a.m. One guy tells the other that he is less drunk so he will drive and it's his truck anyway. He is also worried that his buddy will throw up in the truck, so he tells him to get in the back of the open pickup and lie down, which he does, and off they go.

Meanwhile, earlier in the night, a family broke down on the highway. They have been picked up but have abandoned their vehicle in the breakdown lane.

For the final part of this jigsaw, another driver has just left his Christmas celebration, also drunk, so what can possibly go wrong here?

As the pickup truck approaches the abandoned vehicle, the driver is distracted by it and without realizing it, is steering toward it. Having drunk as much as he had, his reaction time is seriously impaired and he can't avoid it. The truck goes over the top of the car, crushing the roof. The guy in the back of the pickup is thrown into the air and miraculously lands on the highway on his feet alive. Meanwhile, the blue car coming up behind sees the accident but not the passenger who flipped out of the pickup truck. What he sees is a man falling from the sky and landing right in front of him. There is no reaction time, drunk or sober, for this man to avoid hitting him, and by the time the car comes to a halt, he has dragged the passenger some fifty yards underneath his car. The man panics and runs off into a nearby field where he is found hiding a little later by police. The victim is lying face-up. We turn him on his side to expose his back for the trauma roll, but he has no back. His back has become a human skid mark down the road.

25

Inertia

Another accident scene, or so we think. We arrive about 7 a.m. The car is wedged between two trees and the area has been cordoned off. About thirty yards around the car, there are brain and bone fragments everywhere.

"What do you want Mick, brai . . . ?"

"Yeah, yeah, Phil . . . I'll go for the skull this time."

The car had hit two trees that were no more than four feet apart, which stopped the vehicle but not the engine, which burst through the front of the car and continued on another thirty feet, coming to a stop in a ditch. Christ, how fast was he going? The victim, a teenage boy, is literally molded to the dashboard and part of the windshield. It takes the fire department forty minutes to cut him out of the car. We bag him with parts of the car embedded in him. He was wearing only a pair of shorts, no seat belt, and the airbag had been removed beforehand. No accident, it would seem.

26

I Get to Die with a Little
Help from My Friends

From probable suicide to "no doubt about it," we are in Marblehead where a gentleman who has had six unsuccessful suicide attempts has succeeded on the seventh. This is not the traditional gun to the head, wrist-slitting, hanging or jumper (all of which I will see in the future) but much more complex, thanks in no small measure to a company called Exit. If you contact them and give them what they consider to be compelling evidence that there is no point in your life continuing, they will send you a video (I'm sure it is also available on DVD and Blu-ray now) with instructions about how to end it all. In this case, the guy was lying on his bed with two propane tanks on the floor. There were tubes going from the tanks to his face, and they were held in place by plastic wrap that encased his head. The pills on the bed may have been to put him to sleep before the propane was turned on.

How could he turn on the tanks if he was asleep? How could he have gotten the tanks in his room, set up the hoses, and covered his head in plastic wrap? I am asking myself these questions because I am staring at a man lying on his bed who has no arms or legs! The video is still in the machine and the police are not looking for anyone else.

Family Cleanup

Up until now, all of the drug-related deaths and reasons given as to why they happened have been in poor neighborhoods. There are, as we know, no economic boundaries related to drug abuse. Where would we be without the arrogance of the upper middle class and the rich who seem to think that a healthy bank balance has given them a higher IQ? Over the coming months, as I listened to the embarrassingly stupid excuses as to why Ms. Penelope had met her end, I wrote down some of the ones I had heard:

She was feeling under the weather last night, so she went to bed early, which translated into she was out of her head and lying on the floor, so we carried her to her room.

We hope you don't think this was a regular occurrence. She was just experimenting. Medical records indicated that she had been experimenting for twenty years.

She wasn't an addict. Careful you don't nick yourself on the needle hanging out of her arm.

We don't know what happened. She was agitated last night and went to bed early. She was particularly bitchy last night and went to her room to snort a couple of lines.

28

Earth Calling Family

We are in Westford at a beautiful house on two acres of land. The family members are present. The girls are crying and the boys are putting on brave faces. The boy victim is in the basement, which has been turned half into an apartment and an entertainment room. Off the main room is the entrance to the indoor swimming pool where the body lies. He is twenty years old with no sign of needles, drugs, mirrors, razor blades, or any of the standard accoutrements that usually belong at this type of scene. The only thing they missed was the cocaine inside his nostrils. The family ask if they can have a few minutes alone with him. The police are suspicious, but we leave the room and one officer stands well in the background but in view of the body, just in case their goodbye isn't the only thing on their mind. The boy's father is not around and an uncle is claiming to be his guardian. The mother is not at the house either. Phil explains that in order to get him released from the ME's office, the next of kin has to sign; in this case, the mother.

"Oh, er, does she?"

He is getting less coherent by the sentence, as are most of them as they start to crash down to earth. It must have been a hell of a party.

"She's in, ah, New Mexico. Yeah, New Mexico."

Enter family backup members 2 and 3:

2: "Yeah, that's right"

3: "Oh right. She is having a problem getting a flight out. She won't be able to get here for a couple of days."

"Yeah," they say in relieved unison. Hmmm. That fooled us. "Can't we fax her signature to you?"

All right now, they're on a roll! Phil informs them they cannot. I am incredibly aggravated with them. I start to answer another question with subtle sarcasm. They are too high to catch on, but Phil does and stops me.

"It's not our concern. Leave that to the detectives."

He's right. People tend to talk to us as if we are part of the decision-making. They are wary of the police because on most of our expeditions, it is a crime scene and there will be accountability, but we are not involved. We are just the removal men. As we leave, I wonder how long it will be before we are called back to this address.

29

Getting Your Affairs in Order

We are going to my third hanging-suicide. This is in an industrial complex and will be the first one that I will participate in cutting down. He is very high up. Most times, as I will find out, they are no more than a foot off of the floor, or even kneeling, a suicide method I will explain later. This guy's feet are level with my head. It is a very elaborate rope system that has him hanging in the center of this huge metal beam. He must have climbed up the side of the beam wall and jumped, swinging himself into the center of the room as there are no boxes, chairs, or ladders underneath him. For added effect, he has a hangman's hood over his head. A detective has tied another length of rope around the trailing piece of rope so that I can reach and take the strain; the idea being that when Phil cuts the rope, our pulley system will allow me to let the body drop gently to the floor. Phil has taped his knife to a long stick and will cut the first rope. We could have waited for the fire department to help, but we already have another call from the ME, so we need to do this quickly. I hope I'm not holding the rope too high. I don't want him to drop and lift me up into the air. As Phil starts to cut the rope, I think how fun it will be to have a body slowly drop out of the sky right in front of me. There are a lot of people watching, many I suspect just to see how this will work, so it's no time for me to be squeamish.

"Take the strain, Mick," says Phil. "He may swing toward you when the rope is cut."

Shit! Not only might I go up in the air as he is coming down, but we might have a midair collision! The rope is cut and none of my crazy notions happen as the extension rope the detective had knotted snapped under the weight and the body came crashing down like a sack of potatoes. Gasps from everyone present, relief for me.

The suicide note he had left was more of an instruction manual and nothing about why he had done it. There was just a list of telephone numbers for people to be contacted, keys to his apartment and his truck, all clearly marked, and instructions about feeding his cats.

The rest of the month consisted of two head-shot suicides, five or six drug overdoses, and an accidental hanging. The hanging was autoeroticism which, if you don't know, is not sex in a car, which is what I guessed when first asked. I know I used to be so innocent. In this case, Uncle Andrew is hanging in a closet, naked. Upon closer inspection of the body, there appears to be underwear marks on his body that resemble bra and panty lines. The underwear is found stuffed in a closet. Family cleanup strikes again!

30

Thanks for the Tip

I am on my way to my first Chinese removal. Phil tells me it will be different from the majority of removals. We arrive in Westford at 2:30 a.m., and we are taking the deceased to a Chinese funeral home in downtown Boston. There is a hive of activity when we arrive. There are at least twenty people. Great-grandmother has passed on, or at least is free of her mortal coil (I'll explain that comment a little further into the story). As we enter the house, we are being videoed by two camcorders. The whole family is there from sons and daughters, grandchildren and great-grandchildren, uncles, aunts, and more continually arriving. Phil explains the procedure to the twenty-something granddaughter who appears to be in charge. There are pots of burning incense wafting through the air and occasionally someone runs screaming through the room. Paper is being put in the pots, which I guessed were prayers or wishes for the great-grandmother. Chinese chanting music was playing on a small tape recorder.

It is an awkward removal as people keep bumping into us, but we finally get her into the hearse. The family asks if they can accompany us down to Boston as such is the acknowledgement of respect for the matriarch. We explain that they can follow us, but they will not be allowed inside when we arrive at the funeral home. Phil asks if they would like us to put the tape recorder in the hearse and continue playing it *all the way to Boston*. They like that idea, so we do it. There is a procession of cars driving down 93 South at forty-five miles per hour with hazard lights flashing following behind us. We arrive at the funeral home about 4:15 a.m. The cameras are rolling again and the family waits outside until we are done. When we come out, each family member shakes our hand and thanks us for the job we did and we are given two decorated red envelopes. Phil explains that this is a tip and part of the tradition and we are one hundred dollars richer. While in the funeral home, we push the stretcher past floor-to-ceiling racks of goodies: computers, clothes, everything you could think of that a person may need/want. I ask what it's all for and he tells me that whatever the person was in life, the family will buy something that reflected that and it will go to the afterlife with them.

31

Security or Playing at It

Hospital runs can be as simple or as exasperating as the security guards make it. We have two hours to get a body to the ME's office where a medical team will be waiting for it. This is a high-profile case and the hospital is twenty minutes away. Plenty of time, you would think. On arrival, we check in with the main desk to get permission to go to the morgue.

"I'll call security," says the receptionist. "They will be right up."

"Great. We have just over an hour and a half to get it back," we say.

"No problem," she replies.

Ten minutes pass and a guard appears. We explain the situation and he goes off to find his partner. It must be a heavy set of keys if it is going to take two of them to open up.

"Now, now, Mick, give them a chance."

Phil informs me that many of the guards don't like to go to the morgue and will find any excuse to delay it even to the point of hoping the next shift will come in and take over the job. Phil tells me the most popular excuses while we wait. Number one is they have a psych patient coming in who may need restraining. The first guard returns.

"We've got a psych patient coming in, so you guys will have to wait."

This guy is not in shape and looks to me like he couldn't restrain too much. He certainly hasn't restrained from too many doughnuts. Another half hour goes by and we are down to thirty-five minutes, still doable but tight. I can hear a TV, so I follow the sound. The Red Sox are playing and who's watching? Yes, our two boys.

"Guys, we have half an hour to get this body to Boston."

"Well, we have been watching the Sox game for the last half hour. Why didn't you tell us?" says the guard.

In the calmest voice I can manage, I tell him that I did tell his partner.

"Well, he didn't tell me, and anyway we have a psych patient coming in."

Twenty minutes left. We go back to the hearse. The guards walk outside waiting, we assume, for their patient. Phil calls the ME's office in full view of the guards. He tells me sometimes this works if they think that we are talking about them to a higher authority as it might bring them back to life. Sure enough, out of a spark of conscience, a tiny flicker of brain activity or with their belief that the call may get them in trouble, they motion us over. The office understands the problem as it is hardly the first time this has happened. We leave dumb and dumber still waiting at the door for their psych patient.

Now please don't think this is typical of all guards as it is not. We have dealt with really good ones too, but I'm relating the experiences I had while doing this job.

32

Brave Shannon

Another day, another hospital. This time we have the body and are going to the hospital. An elderly lady has died and left instructions to have her body go to medical science. The guard tells us to wait at the entrance as he has to go to the other side or the building to get the key to the morgue entrance. Half an hour later and we are still waiting. We call security again and two minutes later a truck pulls up and out gets Shannon. She is young, enthusiastic, and appears to have a brain in her head. She apologizes for the delay and tells us that the other guard's shift ended and he neglected to tell her we were waiting. Go figure! Phil and I are happy that Shannon is going to help us, but Shannon isn't smiling anymore. You see, Shannon has never seen a dead person, never been to the morgue, and would never like to go there. She was shown where it was, but in her first two weeks of work, this is the part of the job she has been dreading. We take the body out of the hearse. Shannon steps back. The body is in a body bag with a stretcher cover over it. We need to get to the tenth floor to drop it off. The four of us enter the elevator. We put the stretcher against the wall and stand in front of it, making us a barrier between it and Shannon, whose face is notably whiter. We arrive at the floor and her keys don't open the door we need to get into. The nightmare continues for Shannon. A passing doctor has keys that work. I was not prepared for what greeted us on the other side. Phil and I spin around instinctively to see where Shannon is. She stands motionless, her face drained of most of her blood as the room we enter opens up to reveal at least fifty cadavers on tables, four of which were being worked on by medical students. I push the stretcher into the adjacent room and Phil chaperones Shannon in behind me. The doctor looks at the pale white and now trembling security guard.

"I guess the medical profession isn't for you then," he quips. A weak smile and a head shake is the best she can do.

We are fully expecting her to faint as we head back into cadaver-land toward the elevator, but the girl finds strength from somewhere and makes it down with us. By the time we get outside, the color has returned to her face and she is smiling again.

"Goodbye, Shannon. Take care."

33

Liquid Diet

Framingham is our next stop, and we are forewarned that an old man is in a severe state of decomposition. As we arrive at the scene, the police are standing outside, which is always a bad sign. We are greeted by that unforgettable smell as soon as we exit the vehicle. We are presented with another old man who is living the life of a hermit. I am used to the state of the houses that some of these poor souls live in, but this was a man who had weighed 180 pounds in life and now was stuck to the floor by his own fluids. He looked more like a rubber doll than a person, and now weighed only 70 pounds. The maggots are having a field day. Our feet are sticking to the floor. He is bagged and we are out in less than three minutes with a few more seconds to flick off the maggots that had started crawling up our suits, and we are away.

"Phil, we really need a separate cab."

"Suck it up, Shirley."

"Well, at least light up a cigarette."

"Put your head out the window."

"I'll put your head out the window . . . yaddah, yaddah, yaddah . . ."

34

Cigarettes and Suicide Are
Bad for Your Health

Three suicides, two drug overdoses, and two apparent natural causes take up the next three days. "Apparent natural causes . . ." I'm starting to question all the stuff I have been taking for granted.

We are now summoned to a house fire in Lawrence where Kathy has fallen asleep in her rocking chair while smoking a cigarette. From what the detectives can piece together, her dress caught fire and when she woke up, in her panic to raise the alarm, she slipped running to the back door and knocked herself out. The fire reduced her, not to ashes as you might expect, but rather to a life-size bloated plastic doll with no wrinkles (she was in her eighties) resembling this almost caricature version of herself.

There is yet another tragic suicide of an older gentleman who could not live with the loss of his wife. He got hooked on the prescription drugs that were meant to ease his pain. He overdosed and as the effects of the drugs started to kick in, he slashed his wrists. We don our suits again as a room that had been painted white was awash in red.

35

Housekeeping

I thought I had witnessed the worst house conditions I could possibly see, but like they say, "never say never." The story is a familiar one: an old man living on his own, refusing help from the neighbors, is lying dead inside his own front door. As we arrive, there is a blue tarp covering the roof. We have to go into the house from the rear as he is blocking the front entrance. It is a tough entry; there are newspapers and junk mail going back years, piled up, three to four feet high. After climbing over the initial barrier, there is a small path no more than a foot wide. The floor is soft under our feet due to the wet newspapers which have been trodden on over the years, mixed with spilt liquids, pet feces, and rain dripping through the temporary tarp on the roof which, it turns out, has been there for two years.

The walls of newspapers are now head-height and the house is more like a maze. We move from the kitchen to the hallway. The stairs are filled with the same junk. There are soaking-wet newspapers where, during the bad rainstorms, the water has flooded down from the bedrooms. There are also rat's nests and old cat food cans. I don't believe he has been able to go upstairs for a long time. His toilet is a bucket to the left of the front door. There is no electricity, yet there are all kinds of weird and wonderful creatures here; some you can see and some are underneath, making it look like the junk mail and newspapers are moving on their own. He is lying half-naked in front of us. One of the guys we work with comments that he will write a book about his experiences and call it *Why Do People Always Die Naked?* Well, they don't always, but many seem to! I don't believe he ever wrote that book.

I kept notes about my experiences, which is why I can recount the stories now in such detail. This particular older gent had refused surgery on a groin problem which, over time, had produced a growth which, without exaggeration, was the size of a basketball between his legs and was currently covered in blood. I can't be sure (as we never heard about the results of autopsy reports), but it looked like it had exploded. There is so little room in the house that we can't get a stretcher in, so we move the man from in front of the door and bring the stretcher to the porch. The police tell the neighbors, who are all outside of the house, that we will be removing him in full view, so if they don't want to see him, they should go back into their homes. Everyone leaves, but as we begin the removal, many curtains are moving as such is the human curiosity for the macabre.

36

Hoarders

Hoarding has come into the spotlight on TV documentaries and some of the regular series programs. Lately, the ones I have seen show people who hold on to all the possessions they have accumulated in their lifetime or at least from the time this compulsion started. In some cases, I have witnessed the individuals have held on to everything that they have brought through the door or that has been mailed to them.

In this case, the house we are in is lined from the floor almost to the ceiling in neatly stacked papers, magazines, and junk mail in a very organized paper maze. I would estimate that this man has been collecting for twenty years or more, judging by the dates on some of the newspapers. And where is the body? Yes, on top of one of the mountains in the dining room. He is within inches of the ceiling. We try climbing up the paper, but it is like walking up cascading snow or sand. It's hard to keep our footing. We finally make it up. I bump my head half a dozen times on the ceiling. There is nothing we can do with him up there, so we grab his ankles and slide/surf him down the paper mountain until we reach the door and bag him.

One Mistake

The following month produces a record number of bodies for us, out of which only two stand out from the ordinary.

We are called to the most northern part of the state. It's November and the weather is getting cold. A workman has fallen from a tower from two hundred feet. He was a twenty-two-year-old male who had just come up from the South, and it was his first and last day on the job. We are not allowed to remove him as we are waiting on OSHA, who seem to be taking their sweet time getting here. Just looking up at where he fell from is making me nauseous. The force of the fall has bent an aluminum walkway above us in half. He is badly crushed, but his heavy clothing gives the appearance of him being intact. The only visible damage is his right hand and wrist, which we surmise he put out in front to try and protect himself. Oh please, God, let him have lost consciousness before that impact! OSHA finds that one of the safety harnesses had not been connected properly. After they are gone, we very carefully put him in the body bag so as not to let his distraught workmates see how badly broken he is.

38

Just in Time for the Train

It is suicide time at the Woburn train station. A man has jumped in front of a commuter train. Now let me say this: If you are going to jump in front of anything, in order to ensure your demise, a train is absolutely the way to go. The train is not going to brake or swerve out of the way to avoid you and/or possibly cause the death of an innocent bystander. There is the usual blood, brains, and gore for about a hundred yards on the track as well as some teeth on the platform. As we leave the tracks with the job done, an officer asks if we get paid a lot of money for doing this. Phil intimates that we do but, to be honest, we don't get paid close to what we should for what we see and do; but with all the removals we do, plus Phil's embalming, he does make a very good living.

'Tis the Season

During the Christmas and New Year season, there is a record amount of bodies to remove. The month of December alone produced thirty-three. You see, this is the season for suicides for lonely people with no one to care about them. Whether or not that is their own fault or not, few people should die alone. It is a time for reflection for me. I have become somewhat cynical over the past few months with the amount of substance abuse–related deaths that I have witnessed and the families with whom I now share little or no emotion, inwardly anyway. We are professionals. There is no hint of disdain from us when we are at a scene. I don't speak of the moms and dads who have lost their babies, but rather the friends that have done their part over the years to bring these "babies" to a premature end, as it is usually these people who are at the scene and not the moms and the dads of the deceased.

40

A Day Off?

I jest of course, as there is no such thing as a day off when you are juggling two jobs especially when one of them has you on call 24-7! Some people have no consideration and just think they can die any old time they like! Nonetheless, I am going with this illusion that I will be able to take my car in to get an inspection sticker. This includes a nice breakfast at home, not at a Dunkin Donuts, Burger King, or Mickey D's. It's a gorgeous day; Barclay James Harvest is wafting through the Bose speakers in the truck. My god, Galadriel must be one of the most beautiful songs ever written. This fantasy lasts just about an hour; enough time for me to eat without rushing.

"Hey, Phil, what's up?"

"I was wondering if you wanted to come out on the boat for the day. We could fish, drink beers, and barbeque whatever we catch later."

"Wow, really?"

"*No,* not really. Murder-suicide in Chelmsford," and away we go.

A woman has been stabbed to death by her boyfriend who then turned the knife—yes, knife—not gun, on himself. He is rushed to the hospital but dies on the way. This is sensitive as the boyfriend is the son of a local cop. There is much tension. Many of the local cops and the media are there before us. We have to almost fight our way through the crowds.

Inside, the female has multiple stab wounds all over her body. This was an angry killing. She was at the bottom of the stairs. The blood trail started upstairs, but she had managed to make her way downstairs to call the police before she died. We have her in the body bag and strapped to the stretcher. This needs to go as quickly and smoothly as possible. There are already rumblings outside. The cops don't want the media there. The detectives inside tell us that they will make sure there is an unobstructed route to the hearse. Phil says it must be quick without seeming rushed. A few minutes go by and the detective gives us the okay to move. The door is opened and we are halfway down the path before the media realize what is happening. Suddenly there is a barrage of TV lights and cameras are on us. People are yelling questions at us. *Why are they asking us?* I think. It takes us only about thirty seconds from the house door to closing the hearse door. It could not have gone smoother.

"What would have happened if we had tripped Phil?"

"I don't think we would have been allowed back in Chelmsford," he says as we speed away.

Catching the media off guard was fun.

41

Batteries Not Included

A number of very unimaginative deaths follow. My god, how weird am I getting, yet this is what I'm thinking when we pull up outside a downtown Boston apartment building. We do removals "out of our territory" when the company whose area it is, is not available. An old lady has died in her bed. She was in her mid-eighties. She is in the body bag in a heartbeat. Phil is smiling.

"Look," he says. He is motioning toward the bed.

"What?" says Mister Naive.

"Notice anything unusual?"

"Yeah, she had hardly a wrinkle on her face for someone of her age," I say, trying to show him how observant I am. This widens the smile on his face.

"Look again," he says.

Lying on the bed on her side table and on the floor are numerous sex toys. I suppose there is no age limit to keeping yourself satisfied, and apparently, it's good for the skin too!

42

Give Yourself Enough Rope

Now, over the past few months, I have seen some inventive suicides, but this one takes the cake. A gentleman attached a rope to a telephone pole, sat in his car, put the rope through the car window and around his neck, and with a good fifty yards of slack, floored it for a perfect, clean head sever.

Later on, when we returned to the ME's office, I noticed the body laid out on the table and it seemed to be intact. In my naivety, I inquired if they had sewn the head back on.

"No," says the tech as he picks up the still severed head and slides it back and forth while singing "I ain't got nobody . . ."

Well, there has to be some lighter moments working there!

As we head toward the exit, we see a body. Even though it is covered with a white sheet, we know instantly who it is. A few days earlier, a man was arrested for thrusting a machete into this victim. The newspaper report originally gave the basic facts and comically (to me anyway) finished with the line ". . . this is not the first time the man used a machete on someone." With the machete still sticking out of the victim and the sheet covering him, what else could I say but "Is that a machete sticking out under that sheet, or are you just happy to see me?"

43

Smells Like Blocked Drains and Teen Spirits

It's a Monday night about 9:00 and we are on our way to a men's rooming house. He has been dead for a couple of days and the smell is the only reason anyone had even noticed he had not been around. We get up to the third floor. I'm carrying a body bag under my arm and we are met by a thirty-something resident. We are waiting outside the room as it is so small, and we need to wait for the police to finish their part so we can go in. He seems a little antsy.

"Wow. Is that a body bag?" he says.

"Yes it is," I retort with vigor.

"I've only seen them on TV. Can I touch it?"

"Err . . . okay."

"So you guys are famous?"

"Yes, we are," I say. Phil turns away, shaking his head. I continue to amuse myself.

"Do you know the Miami guys?" he says.

"We've spoken on the phone," I say.

"Yeah, those women are gorgeous. Do you think you will ever meet them?"

"Well, if we have an interstate homicide, there's a good chance."

Phil's heard enough, but before he can drag me away by my ear, a young guy comes into the building. It's my guy's friend.

"Great news," he yells up. "I've got the booze."

"Even better news," he yells back. "That smell wasn't the drains blocking up. It's just a dead guy."

My new friend is no longer interested in me as his young buddy and he disappear into one of the rooms.

"How much for an autograph?" Phil asks.

"If you have to ask, you can't afford it, son," I retort.

As we get the motor running and start heading down the highway (feel free to sing along), the next call comes in from the ME's office.

44

The Last Gamble

This is good timing. We are just two exits from where we need to be. A young man has accrued large gambling debts which we are told he felt he could never pay off. He says in his note that it is only a matter of time before they will come for him. He can't keep looking over his shoulder and his addiction won't allow him to stop gambling. He sees only one solution. He is hanging from the ceiling in the basement, still wearing his tool belt from his day job. We cut him down and lay him on the floor. Phil and the detective are talking.

"Check his pockets, Mick. I will be back in a minute," Phil says as he and the detective head upstairs, leaving me alone with a dead body for the first time.

As I put my hands in his pocket, he opens his eyes and asks me what I'm doing. Not really. Just a crazy thought brewing in my imagination! I check both pockets of his jeans and Phil returns much to my relief.

45

Toys Are Us

A short trip to the next town over brings us to Stevie P, a twenty-something-year-old man found in his apartment with no apparent cause of death visible. He is naked. His rabbi had been called to say a few words over the body. He is at a loss as to what happened. He was a good Jewish boy, no drugs, he didn't drink, and no obvious clues of foul play. Surely he was too young for a heart attack. The rabbi continues singing the boy's praises. What strikes me is that the rabbi is here but not the family. After all, it was the family who called him. Hmmm . . . me thinks the family have already been here earlier. Feels like family cleanup again.

But what? No needle marks? The boy is in great shape. Well, for a dead guy. One of the detectives and I start looking around. It's not part of my job, but we have forged a really good relationship with the police. I open a drawer behind the rabbi to find the usual stuff: letters, bills, etc. The same is found in draw two but, goodness me, not draw three. The detective must have seen my surprise. He walks over.

"Anything, Mick?" I move back smiling. The rabbi turns.

"Did you find anything?"

"No," says the detective swiftly as he closes it.

Inside this rather large drawer are leather handcuffs, studded chokers, whips—stuff I have never seen in my sheltered life—and a totally ridiculous-sized dildo. Come on, girls and boys! How can we compete with that? I leave the room, quickly holding back the laughter. I could surmise and give my theories as to what happened, but hey, let's make this reader participation.

46

Careful What You Wish For

It's 2 p.m. on a Tuesday afternoon. I have finished my full-time job early so I take the opportunity to get that inspection sticker that is many months overdue. I am scanning through the local paper and I come across the story of a man who has apologized to three families whose little girls he has molested. I bet that went over well. I think how strange it seems to me that he would apologize for what seems to be no reason, at least none that is given in this story. If he has just been sentenced, it might make sense, but this guy is not in jail? He had told the families that he had no control over his actions. His urges simply overwhelmed him. Give me five minutes with him and we will see how overwhelmed he gets, or even better, give those families a few minutes with him. I didn't get five minutes with him, I got fifteen.

A phone call comes from Phil. He picks me up from the garage and we are on our way to pick up this very same guy I was just reading about. Well, at least my car will have a new sticker when I get back. This guy had told his mother the same thing he told the girls' families, and then took a large overdose of heroin as he could see no way of living his life with any normalcy and without endangering other children. His mother was heartbroken. It's strange how you never think, or feel, for the families of people like him. I suppose I wouldn't have either if I had not seen her.

47

The Great Outdoors

Spring is on the way: a change of seasons, but no change of schedule.

"Want to pick one up in the woods?" says the man on the other end of the phone.

"Sure I do." After all I was only sleeping.

It's only three miles away but on a very busy road. We pull up behind the cruiser. Cars and trucks are whipping by us. There is no breakdown lane. As we open the back of the hearse, I have one eye on the equipment we need to get out and one on our ever-vigilant motorists who might plough into the back of us at any moment. Incredibly, there are motorists (and I use that term very loosely) beeping at us. Another cruiser pulls up behind us, which makes me feel a little safer, and finally the goons who have licenses to drive their two tons of hurtling metal catch on to the situation and stop beeping. Fortunately, there are few trees with foliage. We are trekking into the woods and could have problems finding our man. We navigate our way up a hill and around numerous obstacles to arrive at a tent city of sorts. There are ten to fifteen tents. People are living here. It's a little community. There are bikes and supermarket trolleys padlocked to trees next to their "owners" tents. Our "client" has a two-person tent. We are told he was a glue-sniffer. The crime scene team believes that the fumes from the glue and the oil heater he has inside the tent overwhelmed him and caused him to suffocate. His jeans and under-pants are down by his ankles. Hey, it can be a lonely life in the great outdoors! We take him up hill and down dale and over the barrier to the hearse. Eighteen-wheelers are barreling by creating enough wind to almost knock us off our feet.

"Let's get the hell out of Dodge," I say as a shudder runs down my spine.

48

Overstaying Your Welcome

It has been a quite month for the business. Phil has had nineteen cases of which I did three, but that's about to change. We are on our way to Methven. A fifty-year-old man has been found dead, wait for it . . . naked, in a neighbor's yard, underneath the stairs leading up to an aboveground swimming pool, by their eleven-year-old daughter. It was hard to estimate how long he had been there as his body had only become visible when the snow started to melt. Now that must have been one hell of a pool party last summer! It has taken the distraught girl three hours to calm down enough to explain how she had discovered it. His clothes have now been discovered in another yard and a homicide is starting to become a distinct possibility. We have been sent there prematurely as the crime scene team has not arrived yet.

Phil gets a phone call from a funeral home. They want him to embalm a body. He calls Harry in the second hearse to meet us halfway between the funeral home and the scene. I hop in with Harry and go back to Lowell while Phil drives back to do the embalming. This time it is good timing. We arrive back as the crime scene team is finishing up. No sign of trauma. We bag him and as we are wheeling him to the hearse, the local newspapers arrive and take a couple of shots of us, which makes the front page on the next day. Phil tells us he is done too and another call comes from the ME and our plans change again. We meet up and I jump back in with Phil while Harry carries on into town to drop off the body. This could be one of those days when we are out for ten or twelve hours straight.

49

Not-So-Easy Rider

We have been sent to a motorcycle accident, which has closed a major highway. There is a backup from closing the road down and Phil drives down the breakdown lane. There are cars beeping at us, giving us the finger, and trying to prevent us from passing them. You might think how mindless that is, but to be honest, drivers here are sick of people who do this on a regular basis just to get ahead in the line. Phil gives no explanation to motorists nor does he put on hazard lights. He could have called the officer in charge and had an escort, but he didn't. Why? Because he enjoys pissing them off. This accident happened because two young bikers decided it would be fun to do wheelies on the highway together and, as you might expect, with one trying to outdo the other, one lost control and is now dead. We pass the media who are back some fifty yards from the scene. This causes a frenzy of activity from them as they have had nothing to do for half an hour or so. One bike is on the side of the road, intact. The other is in pieces on the road, in the breakdown lane, on the grass, and some bits in the trees. Such is the devastation that speed can cause. I can see the body. It is wrapped, literally, around a tree. There is a jacket, gloves, and various other pieces of debris scattered around. What looks like the leg of his jeans is hanging in the tree. *As long as his leg isn't in it,* I think, but it is. It was torn off like a turkey leg. We suit up, which increases the media's attention, but they are too far away to get a good view of the gore. Everything is removed. We do one final check and Phil sees a piece of intestine hanging off a tree. It is removed and we set off.

As we head into town, Harry calls. He was sent to a hospital to pick up another body. Now if you are wondering how he can do that on his own (without an ankle man), it is because the body is already in a body bag, so it is just a case of sliding it onto the stretcher and loading it into the hearse. When he gets to the other end, he can get one of the ME's people to help him unload or, in this case, us, as we arrive there within minutes of each other. The other reason only one person is required is the size or weight of the body, and I am happy to say I have never been required to be present to remove a baby or a young child.

There is only one tech on duty right now, so we help remove the clothes from our motorcycle victim and put them in bags. We take off his jeans. The other leg is barely intact. He is down to his under-pants. The body is a bloody mess and the tech gets his scissors to cut the pants off. This happens a lot when there is so much blood. He cuts the pants but inexplicably pulls them before they are cut all the way through (he must have thought they were). You have probably seen or heard about the people who study blood splatter patterns to help determine the angle a knife or gun was at when inflicting the fatal blow on a victim. Well, this blood splatter was no mystery. The pants snapped and Phil and I were showered in blood. Phil has spare T-shirts. We quickly wash our hands and faces. Fortunately, both of us wear glasses so none gets in our eyes. We go straight home, put the clothes in the laundry and shower.

50

We're So Sorry, Uncle Albert

A routine case, an older man dead on his kitchen floor. There is no electricity, so we go in with flashlights. There are three cops inside. One is on his first day out of the academy and is getting ribbed mercilessly by the other two. He has never seen a dead body before. He is in the house but won't go into the room where the body is. A few seconds in and we realize that this is not ordinary. This story is not about his death but rather about his life.

The house is bachelor-style, messy, not awful, but you still wouldn't want to live there. His kitchen consists of a table, two chairs, and a cooler for a refrigerator. His stove is an outside barbeque grill. There is a whole wall of car batteries, floor to ceiling high, for power. I have never seen anything like it. As we take him out to the hearse, a neighbor approaches. He has rosary beads in his hands and asks if we can put them in the bag with him. We have to decline as nothing that was not on the body can be taken with us. The man, holding back his tears, pleads, but we can't. Phil explains the situation to him and tells him that if he brings them to the funeral home, they will put the beads with him.

This is a nice middle-class neighborhood with the exception of this house. It looks as if one good storm would knock it down. The neighbor wants to tell us the story of Uncle Albert. Normally, it is sky-high druggies who want to tell us stories, and we get out as soon as we can. But this is different and we are intrigued. Albert was a frequent visitor to the man's house. He would let him stay in a guest room when it got too cold. Albert had lived his last ten years in the house without any electricity, heat, or running water. Albert was a former soldier and Korean prisoner of war. After he left the service, he was under the illusion (or maybe not) that the government was keeping tabs on him and, at times, following him. He refused to pay taxes and consequently there were many liens on the house. Toward the end, when he left the house, he would padlock it in case "they" tried to get in. The neighbor had large metal cutters that he had bought for Albert at his house. Albert would only use a number padlock and never a key lock because the key could be found. With a number lock, Albert would be the only one who knew the combo locked safely away in his head. But Albert could never remember the combo, so every day he came home, the neighbor would give him the cutters and Albert would have to cut the lock and buy a new one for the next trip. He loved children, and the local kids loved Uncle Albert. I am so sorry, Uncle Albert, that your life ended up this way and you died believing the country you put your life on the line for had hounded and persecuted you.

51

Bates Motel

The Reading Police have contacted the ME's office and asked for us by name. It's always nice when you are asked for by name, and it also lets the office know we are doing a good job.

The old man has been dead for five weeks. We have been told that the police have not gone inside the house yet. We are a little confused. The detectives meet with us and tell us all that they have information from the man's brother and they are expecting a horrendous sight inside. Harry and I are thinking that unless the maggots have got him, he should just be mummified so he will look more like ET than a zombie. We head in and he is indeed mummified and truly does look like ET. The reason for the trepidation with the police was because a fireman had gone in earlier and told everyone that it was a horror show, so everyone took his word for it. All I can think is that it was the fireman's first body. The old man had been found by his brother who had flown in from California as a surprise visit. The reason for suspicion in this case was because the son was living there and hadn't reported his father's death. The son is mentally challenged and the sad reality was that he had had an argument with the dad and thought his father was mad at him and had just stopped talking to him. The son had been bringing the dad his meals for five weeks and then taking them away when he hadn't eaten them.

52

All for Love

It's a beautiful April morning. The phone rings.

"Wanna pick one up off the beach in Marbleherd?"

Of course I do; it's our hometown. He can't be more than three minutes away from us wherever he is. The man is sitting on a lobster-pot with his back against the seawall. He must have been there before dawn drinking a bottle of vodka and watching the sun rise one last time before he put a gun under his chin and blew half his head away.

Apart from the gun and the empty bottle of vodka, the only other thing in his possession was a picture of a woman. He was fifty-one years old but he looked a lot younger. How strong the power of love must be to drive you to this. There seems to be a strange logic in the minds of people who commit these kinds of suicides. Some of the notes I have seen or been told about indicate that they are trying to get back at the person who shunned them, the "I'll show her" or "she'll be sorry now" syndrome. Really? She'll be sorry? Well, she may be, but she'll get over it. There's no way back for you!

53

What Not to Wear

On our way back from the ME's office, we have to call in at a funeral home to embalm and dress a body for a wake. She is a twenty-nine-year-old car accident victim. She is badly broken up and after the postmortem, she is a real mess. Not for the faint of heart this one. The one saving grace here is that her face has not been disfigured. It normally takes Phil about an hour or so to embalm a body, but after a postmortem it takes a lot longer. With a regular embalming, when the body is ready for the embalming fluid, you cut the carotid artery, tie it off at one end, and when the fluid is pumping in the body, the color should begin to come back. If it doesn't, you have to massage the body to get the fluid flowing. When complete, you remove the arterial tube, tie it off at the end, insert it into the upper part of the artery (where the head is), and do the same thing. However, if the body has been postmortem, the arteries have been severed in many places and the procedure I have talked about has to be repeated over and over. I have skipped over some of the details of embalming (remember no dignity in death) as it is quite frankly gross. Yes, gross from the mouth of the man who picks up brains and dismembered body parts. If you really feel the need to know more, you can find the "how to embalm a body" information online. This one takes about four hours. Sewing the torso back up is one thing you have seen on many TV series (the Y shape) with what they call baseball stitching. This girl has had her arms and legs sewn back on and her skull opened, which means her face can be pulled off and then back on like a Halloween mask. I told you it was gross. The family has given the funeral home a beautiful flowing gown for her to wear with see-through chiffon sleeves. If you've seen Stevie Nicks perform with Fleetwood Mac, you know the style I mean. We can't use it because there is so much damage to the girl that the dress will not cover it, so we need to inform the family that a more conservative outfit is required.

We return the next day and a new outfit has been chosen. It is a pantsuit and blouse with a high neckline. It sounds good, but there is more work to be done. She is a size 10, but after all the special plastic undergarments are put on her (this is done in case there are any leaks which could stain the clothes or cause an odor—if you're a good embalmer, this should never happen, but it is a precautionary measure that the funeral homes use), she really needs a size 14. So now so we have to cut the back of the outfit and pin it so that it looks good. The makeup is next. Phil is given a photo of the girl, and he uses it to get as close to the picture as possible. Due to illnesses and the like, some peoples' faces are drawn and barely recognizable to their own family, so he has used Botox on occasion to help fill the face back out.

54

Hourly and Nightly Rates

Phil is away for a few days, so Harry and I are holding down the fort. The first call comes in early Saturday morning: three bodies, all male, all within two miles of each other. This is the first time we have taken two hearses out at the same time. Our first port of call is Route 1, which has a large number of small, dare I say, questionable motels. The scenario is almost the same at drug overdose scenes. The male is lying on the bed. On the table next to him is a cigarette lighter, an elastic tourniquet, a spoon, and the remnants of heroin, cocaine, or whatever choice of drug he decided to poison himself with. We go down two motels to the next scene where we are greeted by the same detectives and cops.

"Hey guys. Haven't seen you for, what, ten minutes?" they say.

It's the exact scene as the one we have just left. This time we are all on the same page, so we are going to leave for the third scene together. As we are about to depart, an argument breaks out between what we had thought were a couple who were standing by the office. The male cuffs the female across the back of her head. The officer walks over and asks the girl if she is okay and if she wants to press charges. She declines. As it turns out, it is a john and a hooker. The john, who looks like he had been partying with the guy we have just put in the hearse, ignores the detectives and in front of all of us asks the clerk how much for a room.

"Forty-five dollars a night," he replies.

"How much for an hour?" he asks.

"Forty-five dollars a night, *SIR*," repeats the clerk.

We leave, shaking our heads. The third overdose is the same, except the body is in the kneeling position. He is not in full rigor, so it is not hard for us to get him on the bed and straighten him out before removal.

55

The Final Toast

Phil is back and Reading is the next destination. One of the town's more colorful characters, a homeless man whom the police are very familiar with, is lying on an old sofa with countless empty bottles of vodka strewn all around. "He was one of those loveable rouges," recalls one of the officers. No matter how many times he was arrested and put in the towns "overnight" accommodation, he had never turned violent and, when sober, would tell anyone who listened that he loved the life he led and would never want to sleep indoors except, he said with a smile, when the town insisted. There is a wooden fence between the garage and the road which hides the scene from the young school children happily playing some fifty yards away.

56

Speechless

We are now in Chelsea and possibly in the seediest motel I have ever seen. The lighting is so low we almost need flashlights to find our way. The corridors inside of the property are bathed in hazy red and orange lights as is the room. The policeman is none too friendly either. I guess he just wants to get to hell out of there too. A young prostitute—no older than eighteen, I would estimate—is lying naked from the waist down with bodily fluids on her thighs and an array of drugs on the bed.

Such degradation I have not seen before. The people in the adjacent room told us she had four male visitors that afternoon. The policeman steps outside to answer a call. When he comes back to the room a minute later, we are moving the stretcher out. "You're done already?"

"Yes. Have a good night, officer."

Phil and I never spoke during the removal or said anything about what we had just witnessed.

57

Just Call Us Hollywood

A man has committed suicide by hanging himself from a tree in the woods in Lynn. He had been fired that day from his job as a town worker for stealing prescription drugs from the medicine cabinet of a house where he was working. He had told his coworkers that he could never tell his wife that he had lost his job because she would kill him. He left work that day, went home, and told his wife he was taking the dog for a walk. When he did not return home, his wife called the police who, in turn, called his workplace and told them the story. He was found after an extensive search at about four in the morning. We were there at five just as dawn was breaking. He is in a dense part of the woods and is swaying slightly in the breeze from a branch about a foot off the ground. The swirling mist and the headlights of the cruisers made this a horror movie producer's dream. Just roll the cameras; done in one take. A couple of detectives ask how we are going to go about this. Everyone else is keeping their distance. It really is a macabre scene. Phil and I know he is in full rigor. We put the body bag on him up to his neck and zip it up while he is still hanging. He winks at me and tells me to steady him when he cuts the rope and explains what we are going to do.

He cuts the rope and the body drops and stands perfectly upright. Gasps come from those assembled. They were expecting him to crumple to the ground. Phil zips the bag up completely, takes a step back and lets him fall into his arms. I grab the feet end and in one seamless movement, we have him off the tree and onto the stretcher. It was brilliant. I'm waiting for applause (or at least "and that's a wrap" from the producer), but everyone is stunned. They just don't appreciate showmanship. Finally, as we are wheeling him to the hearse, a couple of cops laughingly call us jerks for scaring the shit out of them but agree they have never seen a better removal in their lives.

58

One Way up, One Way Down

We are in Waltham. There is going to be no throwing this guy over your shoulder and curtseying for the applause. He is 370 pounds. Phil is asked by the ME's office if we need a third man. He says no as he is clearly on a high from the last removal.

This town has a huge one-way road system and my friend here is getting annoyed with it. We find the street, which is a one-way, and we are, of course, at the wrong end of it. Or are we? I know that look on Phil's face as we head into oncoming traffic.

"What?" he asks. "We're only going one way." This is not an ordeal for him. He likes it.

The police ask if we will want the fire department to help get the body down.

"Not necessary," says Hercules.

It is a very humid day and that's bad. He is five stories up and that's very bad. He is 370 pounds and that's very, very bad, and we haven't surveyed the scene yet. Our shirts are already soaked through with perspiration. When someone is up on a higher floor, you ask a lot of questions before you go up so you know what equipment is necessary. You only want to go up and down those steps once.

"Are you sure you don't need help, guys?" asks the officers again.

Yes, we need help, I say to myself. Bring the whole department. Bring the coast guard, bring lawyers, guns, and money. The next line in that Warren Zevon song was very appropriate to this situation. The man had a very bad case of diarrhea when he died and indeed the shit had hit the fan, the floor, and in fact everything within a ten-foot-square area.

"No thanks," says Superman. "We will be fine."

Is it a bird, is it a plane, is it a nutcase? No, it's a big show-off boss man. I can see the cops are skeptical. Having resigned myself to the fact that this was going to happen, I had a sudden change in attitude. Yes, it will be a challenge, but we really are pretty good at this so, *Yes, we can.* This sudden change in my mental attitude was crucial if I wasn't going to let Phil down. We bring up two body bags, extra belts, and hazmat suits. We are almost ankle-deep in excrement. He is too big for one bag, but with the two bags and the extra belts, we should be able to hold him together.

"Mick, we can do this," Phil assures me.

"I know we can," says this born-again optimist.

We need to get him out of the room before we bag him. I don't want us trailing crap down the stairs and into the hearse. It is my job to pull this colossus of a man with the straps out to the hallway. I pull him about ten feet and look at Phil.

"Don't think I don't know what you're doing," he assures me.

Good, because it is all I can do, but Phil's confidence spurs me on and he is out on the landing. We have to deal with the balancing problem (namely, his huge belly). I was wondering why he had not done the pulling. He always took the heavy end. After we had secured him, I found out why. He was saving his strength for the stairs. I had to pull from the front, but he was the brake man and would have to take the strain for the five flights of stairs which are, in fact, ten flights of stairs. It is a monumental effort, but twenty minutes later we are down. We load him in the hearse, draining the last of our strength.

"Don't make it out to be a big deal in front of them, Mick," he says as we are about to leave the scene. The cops' skepticism has turned to admiration.

"Amazing," says one.

"All in a day's work," replies Mr. Cocky Pants, and we leave.

59

The Family

We are in the projects in Salem and the father of a very well-known family around these parts has died in his sleep. Because the family is so "well known," the police want to rule out foul play. This is not the kind of neighborhood your molly-coddled storyteller here is used to. There are bricks and garbage on the street and old cars in driveways that look like they are being used for spare parts. I really do not want to get out. There is a crowd of about twenty people gathered outside. Phil looks at my face.

"Yes, you middle-class snob. We do have to get out of the hearse."

There is a lot of screaming and yelling going on in and outside of the house. A detective meets us as we walk up the path.

"Sensitive situation here, gentlemen," he tells us.

No shit, Shakespeare. As we walk up the narrow staircase to the bedroom, we hear hysterical screams. It is his wife, and she doesn't want to leave the room. When she sees us, she goes into overdrive. The police are having no luck with her and she is not leaving the room. Furthermore, the bastard sons of bitches (that's us) are not taking him anywhere. Phil takes control. He asks the family to help and asks the police to go downstairs.

Their two daughters and three sons are present. The daughters take the mother into an adjoining bedroom. The three sons are standing in the room silently. None of them are less than six-foot-three and built like the proverbial brick outhouse, and I'm thinking they could snap us like twigs. That is the last thing on their minds. Two are holding back tears and one can't. We prepare the father for removal and Phil asks the sons if they want to help take their father down to the hearse. Their faces brighten up as they no longer feel helpless. At the much calmer mother's request, we leave the body bag partially unzipped so she can say her goodbye. A minute or so later, Phil and the sons are taking him down. As we get outside, the mother loses her temporary composure again. When he is safely in the vehicle, Phil answers the family's questions about what happens next. The mood outside is still very tense as different rumors are circulating as to how the man died. Phil's experience has made a potentially explosive scene go very smoothly. This is a good time to leave, he tells me. Really? I thought that before we got out of the hearse.

60

Posthumous Introductions

We respond to quite a few colleges. It's about a fifty-fifty split between suicides and overdoses (of course there are the occasional accidental deaths). Today it's both. There's a suicide on campus where a young male had emailed his mother and told her what he was about to do. She called the police immediately and although their response time was within minutes, they were still too late. The mother was blaming herself, as parents do, for not seeing the email sooner, yet as the time of death and the time the email was sent were so very close to each other, it seemed like he had taken his life immediately after he sent it.

Amazingly, while we prepare to leave, we get another call for the same college, this time a drug overdose off campus, one hundred yards away from where we are. A nineteen-year-old male is dead on the floor in a basement apartment. He is the only person there who is not a student. Several young girls from the party are crying. A year or two ago, I would have felt sorry for them and would have had words of comfort, but not now. They were partying with OxyContin, speed, and vodka. I just want to shake them and ask them what the hell did they think was going to happen—it's not the '60s; this is thirty-plus years later. There cannot be anyone alive who doesn't know what danger a mix of drugs and alcohol can bring. Ironically, the deceased was the one who supplied the drugs. We load the second body in and Phil quips, "Wayne, this is Steve. Steve, this is Wayne."

61

The High Life

A good number of removals occur in high-rise apartment buildings. This can present its own problems. Most of them have elevators (if they're not out of order) and those vary in size. Most apartment buildings have small elevators; after all, they're not hospitals where they are designed to transport live people horizontally. So, on many occasions, we have to stand the stretcher vertically, empty or full. It is always interesting to see people's reactions when we are on our way down with a body.

After the initial shock, the vast majority just tell us they will catch the next one while stepping back a pace or two, but not all. I have had them ask us to get out when we arrive at their floor or ask why we can't take the stairs. One guy asked us that on the thirtieth floor. My reply encouraged him to wait for the next one. One lovely lady who had two young children in tow came running toward us after we had stacked a body in and asked us why we couldn't wait for the next one.

"We need to get the body down quickly," I said.

"Why? This one is in no hurry," she retorted, nodding to the body.

"No, but we are," replies Phil.

"You're welcome to come down with us," I say sarcastically, and in she comes dragging the bewildered kids with her.

Clue

A puzzling one here: a lady in her mid-sixties, lying on the floor with a telephone cord around her neck and a weighing scale next to her. What happened? Did she trip over the scale and accidentally catch her head in the phone cord and choke? Did someone come up behind her and strangle her with the phone cord? Was she talking to someone on the phone, have a heart attack, and fall into the cord? Was she on the phone listening to someone's boring conversation, thought she would step on the scale, saw how much she weighed, and hung herself? Or was it Miss Linda in the library with the candlestick? We may never know. It could always be a mystery.

63

Mary, Mary Quite Contrary

We have been out all day with nothing out of the ordinary, for us anyway. It is 3:30 in the afternoon and we haven't eaten since breakfast.

"Where now?" I ask.

"Belmont" is the reply.

"Really? That's excellent! How do you fancy the best fish and chips you've ever eaten? My cousin Frankie has a fish store in the center of town and after the removal, we can get treated to a free lunch."

I know there is no such thing as a free lunch, and halfway through lunch we are heading to Rowley and a trailer park. One of the local female characters in the park has overdosed. There are more police then usual here.

"What's the big deal?"

"No big deal," says one of the officers. "It's just that every one of the guys in the department has had a run-in with her at one time or another and there are a few of us who want to pay our last respects."

"Or just make sure she is dead," quips another.

"Yeah," says another, as he and a few of the others hold back their obvious delight.

Over time you meet a lot of the same detectives. One of our favorites is here today.

"Gentlemen, let me introduce you to Mary. Mary has said some terrible things over the years about the department and our captain—mind you, a lot of it was true. I've told the boys how good you are at getting bodies in awkward places out quickly."

Okay, I think. What can the problem be? It's a trailer. This trailer has two levels and the second level is only about four feet from the ceiling. That is the bedroom, and with the mattress diminishing the height, there is just enough room to lie down. I don't care for confined spaces myself, and the woman who was in her mid-forties is lying on the mattress, legs spread, naked from the waist down. It is a little embarrassing as we have no choice but to crawl up on the bed with her. Now there is all kind of comments flying around.

"That's enough," says the captain, who made a special appearance himself.

Phil thinks that the best approach is to have the bag ready on the floor and tip the mattress forward so she is upright and we can then slide it up her body, allowing us to bag her without having to do it outside the trailer. It works! What a treat!

"I told you they were good," our detective friend says.

64

Here Is an Offer We Can't Refuse

I have pretty much seen everything by now but a murder in our sleepy little town, and on top of that, a mob hit? It doesn't seem real, but that is what we are being told by our local detectives. Mr. Clayton of Marblehead, formerly of Boca Raton, formerly of Los Angeles, formerly of . . . well, you get the picture. He has been moved around a lot, but they have finally caught up with him. We are about to enter the house when a call comes in from the ME. We are told to leave the scene and head to Braintree where a body has washed up onto the shore, but not before they mentioned our friend Mr. Clayton had been tied to a chair with a bullet in the back of his head. The detectives think it is a young man who fell overboard from a fishing boat one week earlier. The story had been headline news for a while. This is crazy! We are at a scene on the North Shore. It is Friday evening rush hour, and they want us to drive forty miles to the South Shore! Phil tries to reason with them but to no avail.

The traffic is as you would expect on a Friday at four heading into Boston. There are three rotaries we have to navigate in order to get to the highway. They are clogged—well, for some anyway. We have no police escort, no flashing lights, but what we do have is Phil.

"Hang on to your knickers," he says as he mimics one of my colloquial lines.

Up on the sidewalk, we go past all these very, very pissed-off motorists. Did we go through red lights? I don't know. I was only interested in self-preservation at that point. What should have taken us an hour or so to get through the city is now completed in twenty-five minutes, but we still have to get to the South Shore. We make the whole trip in an hour and a quarter, but that is only the beginning of our problems.

The area we are in is desolate. No real roads, just sandy tracks, and we get directed to the wrong side of the bay. After half an hour or so, we find the right side and again are given wrong directions. This time we are pulling up to where the distraught family is standing, hoping against hope that it is not a body, and if it is, that it is not their son. The mother sees us and breaks down.

"You're not supposed to be here," says a local cop.

Everyone is pissed at the time this has taken, and we are the object of their anger. Phil, who is always calm in these situations, has had enough too.

"Do you think we could follow someone who knows the area?" A cop takes us.

"Where the fuck have you been?" is our greeting.

We explain the situation, but they are not listening. They have been there for three hours on a cold, windy beach, and they need someone to vent at. Now, while understanding their frustration, there is a limit to the amount of continual abuse and snide comments that we are going to take—and we have reached it. A yelling match ensues. Other more level-headed officers intervene and calm things down. The body, or what the sea has left of it, is lying on a plastic bag. The lead detective, who we think knows the family, wants to come back to the city with us.

"You're not going to stop for lunch on the way, are you?" he says.

As we spin around, there is a half-smile on his face. We find out later that it was in fact the young man who fell overboard.

Lord of the Flies

Although summer is officially over, we have had a week of hot, humid weather, and when we arrive at our next destination, we are told it is a deco. He has been there a week. No one has been in the room because there is a loud buzzing noise coming from it. The best guess is that there is a large amount of flies in there that have not been able to escape. We suit up, this time with face masks and hoods. We know what we have to do: run in the door, close the door behind us, and run to open the windows as quick as we can and hope they aren't stuck. We don't know what to expect, but the landlord gives us a quick description of where things are. We open the door and in we go. It's unbelievable! A black cloud of flies and, oh boy, do they like us! We get four windows open and the screens out in double quick time. The flies like freedom even more than we do! The rest, as they say, was a piece of cake as removals go!

66

Good Night, Good Night, Parting Is Such Sweet Sorrow

Hillary and Tommy were star-crossed lovers, but, as in the bard's tale several hundreds of years earlier, their love could never be. She is Jewish, he is Muslim, and their love means nothing to the two families who will not hear of them dating, never mind marrying. Yes, this is twenty-first century America, but as we are well aware, deep-seated beliefs transcend beyond the happiness of individuals. Their families won't allow them to be together, and they cannot bear to be apart. In their eyes, the only alternative is to leave this world together. We find a knife and their blood-soaked bodies lying in a loving embrace on the bed.

67

Debbie Downer

It's Sunday morning and we are taking another trip to Lynn. I like these calls. We usually spend time finding Dunkin' Donuts to keep us going, but in this town they are everywhere. This is our third visit to this building (which faces Dunkies) in just over a year. It's the same old drug party with the same junkies, some of whom I actually recognize from previous visits. I wonder if they ever think maybe we will be back for them next time.

This time one of the girls collapsed on the floor so to "not put a downer on the party, man," they carried her to the back room to sleep it off.

"She was dead this morning when we went to wake her."

Well, we will have to see what the autopsy report says, but my money is on her being dead when they took her out of the room last night. There is a large crowd outside, many of whom are the party-goers. One of the girl's friends is close to hysterics. As we bring the body out, she screams for us to unzip the bag because her friend can't breathe. Phil obliges. There is no point in engaging in a discussion with a bunch of junkies, half of whom are still high, about the need for a dead girl to be able to breathe.

68

Short Trip

Another trip to Dunkin' Donuts-ville. It is a scorching, hot, and humid day. The young man is a couple of floors up. We are downtown and a lot of people have gathered. There is nothing special about this case. After he is in the hearse, I can't wait to take my plastic gloves off. In this heat. the sweat has nowhere to go. When you remove the gloves, there is almost a cup of perspiration gushing out, much to the disgust of the onlookers, who I am sure think it came from the deceased.

We are standing on a comer in the road chatting with the local cops whom we have gotten to know very well now when a car comes racing around the comer. Phil is right next to the hearse and jumps up onto it while yelling at me to look out. I didn't see the car coming and take a step back. The driver slams on his brakes and the car stops, its bumper touching my jeans. After a few choice words, all the bemused driver can say is, "Well, I didn't hit you, did I?"

"Hey Mick, we had everything in place," says one of the detectives.

Had I been hit and killed, all the necessary people and equipment would have already been there to take care of me! That would have been the least amount of paper work and physical manpower hours ever. Thanks guys!

Chasing the Dragon

A policeman once told me when we were taking another drug-related death out that he had previously asked this same man, whom he had busted on many occasions in the past, why he started using. The guy told him that he tried it once, just to see what it was like (I know, sounds familiar), and that the high he got was so euphoric (his words) that he had to try and get it back again. Each time the high got less and less, so he would take more and more in an attempt to chase after that first time, which he did, until the last time.

Are You Sure, Phil?

With the exception of the car incident, I have never felt that my life was in danger doing this job. I asked Phil if he had because, for some reason, on our way to a removal in an infamous downtown project at 3 a.m., I had a bad feeling about it.

"No," he said, I think sensing my trepidation.

"The people who do this don't want to hang around death."

As we put the unfortunate into the body bag, three bangs ring out in quick succession.

"Just a car back-firing," says the boss.

The police say nothing. Two more ring out. As we are about to leave, one of the cops tells Phil about a different route out. He says it is a little longer, but we should go that way and—like the proverbial red flag to the bull, which way do you think we went?—I was extremely pleased when we hit the highway.

Just Say No

Kevin is a volunteer at a boys-and-girls club. He runs the basketball program and helps kids stay out of trouble and away from drugs. He has all the equipment he needs in his office. He is wearing his Celtics top, shorts, ankle socks, great sneakers, has a bag full of basketballs in the comer, a rubber tourniquet, spoon, lighter, and a bag full of cocaine on the desk. Kevin is also slumped over a chair, dead, with the antidrug poster on the wall above his head.

72

Sharing

There are many organizations that do their best to help homeless people from large shelters transition to single-family homes. Today we are at a well-known shelter for men. The victim is a fifty-something male who is sitting on the edge of his bed, head down, wearing only a pair of underpants. He has either had a stroke, heart attack, or overdosed on something. But there are no drugs, needles, or any kind of indication as to the cause. Casting an eye, we realize he also has no clothes or, in fact, any possessions. There are four beds in this part of the room, and his three roomies stand there lying to our face as to where his possessions have gone. I suppose it is survival for them. After all, we only take what he is wearing and the chances of there being a relative to give his possessions to are slim. In the ME's office, his pants are removed and what falls out? Well, yes, but apart from that, there is also a used syringe and a small plastic bag of heroin. I breathe a sigh of relief for myself and all present that no one got pricked by it.

73

It's Only a Game

Next we are at a small shelter, a single-family house run by one of the nicest guys I have ever met. He has dedicated his spare time to helping people get back on their feet and has opened his home to four people at a time who can stay for up to six months. The house is nice and the rooms are comfortable. The basement has been turned into a game and music room. There are drums, amplifiers, guitars, and keyboards, as well as a pool table, table tennis, darts, video machines, and a hockey table which our victim is lying under. There is a lot of blood on the floor. Today I am with Harry.

The hockey table is heavy, not a ninety-nine-dollar special from a national chain, so coordination is key. When I lift it up on one end, Harry has to pull him out quickly. Five seconds and it is done. The man has numerous slashes to his neck and defensive wounds on his arms. The weapon is under his body. It is the lid to a large coffee can, about six to eight inches in diameter, which, in itself, doesn't seem that menacing, but when it has been opened with a can opener, it becomes more like a kung fu star (remember them), completely serrated. The owner is beside himself, six years and never a problem. Is it possible that this was over a hockey game?

74

Southie

Today we are covering for a Boston removal company. We arrive in South Boston to face a large crowd of people, neighbors mostly. PJ's wife left him earlier in the year, which he didn't think was so awful (as any of the neighbors will tell you), but she won custody of his little boy and that was just too much for him. They have their own way of doing things in Southie, and this style of suicide is no exception.

Punching a hole through the sheet rock wall above an interior door allows you to push a short rope through, tie it around the frame of the door, place a noose around your neck, and then you can slowly start to drop toward your knees and the rope will render you unconscious before death. At that point, your body weight does the rest.

PJ had written two notes, one to his brother Sean and the other to his little boy. It began with "My brave little man, don't think Daddy is mad for doing this, he is just very, very sad . . ." That is as far as I could read before tearing up.

"You are a braver man than me, Mick Lynch" said Phil. "I won't read them and you're not supposed to anyway."

No problem there, Phil. I won't be doing it again.

As we pull away, another phone call comes in. Are you guys still in Southie?

"Indeed we are," says Phil.

A shoot-out between two drug dealers. Not until we arrive at the scene do we realize the extent of the tragedy—only one is dead.

Yes, but It Feels So Good

What grosses me out the most? Blood? Guts? Brains? Decapitation? The smell? Maggots? I'm not sure. They all have their moments! Many of those "moments" we encounter, all at once, on our next assignment. Cam is a 300-plus-pound badly decomposed male who looks like he is moving because there are so many maggots infesting his body. They are crawling in and out of his eyes, nose, mouth, ears . . . well, you get the picture. We get him in the bag and wipe off all the maggots from the outside of the bag that we don't want to bring in the hearse with us. Er, that would be all of them!

When we arrive at the ME's office, there is only one tech on duty, so Phil decides that we should be nice guys and give the tech a hand and help him remove the clothes. The temperature was dropping fast outside and my hands were cold. The rubber gloves that we wear make them feel even colder. Christ, Phil, really?! It was bad enough dealing with maggots once. Now we have to do it again! Well, okay. We unzip the bag and they spill out everywhere. The smell is insane! As I said, he is a big guy, so we have to put our hands right underneath his maggot-squirming body to center him properly onto the slab, and what do I feel? A nice, warm sensation comes over me. The maggots are so warm and my hands are so cold, it felt toasty! My eyes and the logical part of my brain are saying this sucks, but my little hands are saying, "Mmm, warm. Nice." Yes, I know it's weird, but I'm just telling ya.

76

Red Tape, Red Snow

The summer and fall have come and gone and the first snow of the year is on the ground. The eleven o'clock news is on and I am happily drinking a cup of tea, snug and warm next to the fire. There is a breaking news story about an accident involving a train and four electricians who have been working on a railway line near one of the shunting stations. I'm waiting to hear what town this happened in when the phone rings.

"Are you watching the news?"

"Yes, Phil. How many dead?"

"Just the one."

It is freezing, windy, and snowy. A train came out of the station and was put on the same line the electricians were working on. Visibility was zero and neither party saw each other until it was too late. The dead man is under the train. We hang around for a few minutes and are told to go into the shunting station as it is the only place that has any heat. The atmosphere is tense between workers, union reps, and management. Well, nothing new there, I guess.

Another hour passes before the train is reversed and we are given the go-ahead to pick him up. A minute later, someone runs over screaming.

"Don't move! They have forgotten to turn off the live rail!" From which we are standing a foot or so away.

Back into the station which, with its concrete floors, is not such a warm place now. Tempers are becoming frayed as details, true or false, are circulating. We have been here for four hours by the time we put him in the bag. Another hour is spent checking the track for body parts. It is difficult to keep our footing with the snow on the tracks, and finding parts is made harder with the wind blowing the snow, covering up and revealing parts.

"Okay," says the man in charge.

"I don't think we are going to find any more in this weather," and thankfully we get to leave with everyone reasonably satisfied.

All that can be done has been done. This is a case I want to forget. We were so cold. It was a disaster from start to finish, but I won't forget it as it turns out to be my last.

Outtakes

Okay, so I know the way I have chronicled these tales makes it look like we were the ultimate professionals and, quite honestly, in the two years we did this together, I never saw Phil make a mistake. But me, well, that's a different story. Here are three faux pas, fortunately only seen by Phil and one morgue attendant.

While picking up one of the motorcyclists whose body was partially dismembered, I pulled his other leg off. It was almost off anyway and only the jeans he was wearing kept it intact.

Keeping with the appendage theme, a jumper who came down eleven floors the fast way was mangled in a bush. As we are straightening him out, Phil tells me to be careful with his foot as it is turned the opposite way and it might—oops, too late! I am standing there with the man's foot in my hand. Phil then laughingly tells me that I must hold the record for the most abusive behavior toward postmortem bodies.

Last, but not least, we were asked to take out a certain child-abusing priest who had died after a short illness. The news media heard about it and were waiting at the front door. Yes, like we are going to bring him out through the main entrance. We take no one out through the front. Down in the morgue, we slide him onto the stretcher and lift him up. I thought I had let go of the release handles. Well, whether I did or not, the stretcher on my end crashes back down again. After the initial shock, the attendant says, "Pity someone didn't drop him on his head when he was alive."

As we drive out the back exit, I wave to the media. Two of them wave back probably thinking that I was someone they knew. They certainly didn't know we were driving away with their headline news for the evening!

The End Is Nigh

I am coming up to the end of my second year on the job. My full-time job is taking up more of my time and, depending upon where I'm working, I bring a spare set of clothing. It is becoming more difficult if I'm working twenty miles or so away on the South Shore. It is not feasible to get over to a removal on the North Shore in good time, not to mention asking my customers if it's okay to take a couple of hours off to pick up a dead body or two. Phil needs someone more reliable. I can do most weekends, but that wouldn't be fair to someone new.

It has been a fascinating experience for me. I have seen a world my cozy middle-class life would never have afforded me. I have been cured of my phobia of the dead. Having seen how fragile life is, the more I question my own mortality and the more I admire those people who do this job. For me, it is time to move on.